D1065335

Papal Envoys to the Great Khans

G370.A2 R3 1971
Rachewiltz, Igor
PAPAL ENVOYS TO T
HE GREAT KHANS,
1971

VOYS

TO THE GREAT KHANS

by

I. de Rachewiltz

STANFORD UNIVERSITY PRESS
Stanford, California
1971

RITTER LIBRARY
BALDWIN-WALLACE COLLEGE

Stanford University Press
Stanford, California
© I. de Rachewiltz, 1971
Originating publisher: Faber and Faber Ltd, London, 1971
Printed in Great Britain

ISBN 0-8047-0770-7

LC 77-150327

To
INES

Contents

Illustrations

PLATES

MAP

Preface

In writing the present volume for the *Great Travellers* series my main objective has been to set out in a continuous narrative form the story of those medieval friars who, just before and soon after Marco Polo, explored the remote regions of Asia as papal envoys and missionaries. Although their travels involved them in journeys of thousands of miles, quite exceptional in their age and for long after, and although theirs constitute the first recorded diplomatic missions sent by Europe into the Far East, yet so far they have attracted little notice. I have hoped to make them known to a larger public, and have consequently attempted to place the story in the wider historical perspective of East-West relations.

In so doing I have brought together information scattered through many contemporary sources, drawing fully, at the same time, from the learned investigations of my predecessors; it would have been impossible to write this book without the painstaking efforts of several generations of scholars who, in Europe, America and Asia, have laboriously reconstructed this important and dramatic page of our past. To have acknowledged my many debts to these scholars in the traditional form of footnotes and references would have been out of keeping with the general character of this series; I therefore take this opportunity of recording my gratitude to them.

I am greatly indebted to the Australian National University for sponsoring my research trip to Europe in 1966–67 during which I collected much of the source material.

It is a pleasure to acknowledge the assistance received from the following persons and institutions: the Biblioteca Apostolica Vaticana, the Archivio Segreto Vaticano, and Professor Mario Gout; the Library of the Sacra Congregazione de Propaganda Fide; the Reverend Fortunato Margiotti, O.F.M., the Reverend Antonio Sisto Rosso, O.F.M., and the Library of the Pontificio Ateneo Antoniano, Rome; the Reverend C. Schmitt, O.F.M., St. Bonaventura College, Quaracchi-Florence; the Biblioteca Medicea Laurenziana, Florence; the Bibliothèque Nationale and the Cabinet des Dessins, Musée du Louvre, Paris; the Harvard-Yenching Institute, Cambridge, Mass.; the Orientalische Abteilung der Staatsbibliothek Preussischer Kulturbesitz, Berlin; the National Palace Museum, Taipei; the Institute of Oriental Studies, Academy of Sciences, Moscow; the National Library of Australia and the Menzies Library, Canberra; the Library of St. Paschal's College, Melbourne, and the Reverend J. A. Keane, O.F.M.; Professor J. A. Boyle, University of Manchester; Dr. K. H. J. Gardiner, the Australian National University; and the late Dr. F. N. Ratcliffe of Canberra.

My thanks are also due to Professor C. P. FitzGerald, former Head of the Department of Far Eastern History, the Australian National University, whose original suggestion led to the writing of this book, and to Professor George Woodcock, General Editor of the series, for his generous advice and criticism. I wish also to express my gratitude to Mr. M. U. Pancino, Department of Human Geography, the Australian National University, for his assistance in preparing the Map of Asia.

Finally, I owe a special debt of gratitude to my wife, Ines, who checked the whole manuscript and suggested many improvements.

the West a world until then either totally unknown or shrouded in myths and fanciful tales. The friars' progress into Asia caused the displacement and disappearance of many of these imaginary notions. The kingdom of Prester John—one of medieval Europe's most cherished myths—had to recede farther and farther to the east. In the end, short of disappearing altogether, the fabulous priest-king was forced to migrate from Asia to Africa, and it was here, in the Dark Continent, that the captains of Prince Henry the Navigator were still hopefully looking for him in the fifteenth century.

The curious and fascinating story of Prester John can be followed through the accounts of the papal legates and missionaries. I have paid special attention to it as it throws much light on the psychological climate in which the first official contacts between East and West took place.

As we would expect, the Franciscan travellers have also much to say about the heretic and schismatic Christians that they met on their journeys and at the Mongol court. Indeed, their writings are a unique source of information on the diffusion and role of Nestorianism in Central and Eastern Asia.

For these and other reasons the narratives of our friars rank among the most important historical documents of the Middle Ages. Unlike most historical documents they make also fascinating reading, as they were written down or dictated by the eye-witnesses themselves who, by their very training, knew well how to observe their surroundings and describe their experiences.

Unfortunately most of their writings, being less conspicuous than Marco Polo's contemporary account, which is not discussed here, or than the even more sensational *Travels* of Sir John Mandeville, did not attract much attention until relatively modern times. Some of them were not known until the nineteenth century and others were rediscovered only a few years ago. The only one that enjoyed great popularity throughout the ages was Odoric of Pordenone's travelogue, which Mandeville so skilfully and successfully plagiarized.

Since Richard Hakluyt and Samuel Purchas first published in England the relations of Pian di Carpine and Rubruck three and a half centuries ago, many new manuscripts and versions of the Franciscans' narratives have come to light. In the Introductory Note to the Bibliography the reader will find a discussion of the most important texts and translations of these narratives. In quoting from the original sources I have made use of the available translations, but I have at times modified them either to adhere more closely to the originals, or to conform to modern English usage.

Mongol and other foreign names and terms are given in the form found in most current scientific works, but with slight modifications (*ch* for *č*, *sh* for *š*, and *gh* for *γ*), and without diacritical marks except for the umlaut.

In the case of a few well-known proper names I have adopted the more popular spellings, hence Qubilai, Khwarezm and Qaraqorum are written Kublai, Khorezm and Karakorum.

The Chinese names of the Mongol emperors are given in brackets in the Index following their Mongolian names.

I

In Search of Prester John: Europe's Early Vision of Asia

> The Anthropophagi, and men whose heads
> Do grow beneath their shoulders.
>
> *Othello*, I.3

THE JOURNEY OF MASTER PHILIP TO THE KINGDOM OF PRESTER JOHN

In the distant October of 1177 Master Philip, personal physician of Pope Alexander III (1159–81), sailed from Venice on a special mission to the East. His task was both hazardous and delicate, and for this reason the pontiff had chosen him, the most trustworthy person of his entourage, to carry it out.

Philip's final destination was the unknown territory beyond the Tower of Babel, then believed to be ruled by Prester John, that fabulous Christian sovereign of the Three Indies. The papal physician and envoy carried with him a letter of Alexander addressed to 'the very dear John, illustrious and magnificent king of the Indies', in which the pope, after having praised the Oriental monarch for his 'Christian faith and piety' and gently rebuked him for 'pride in his opulence and power', urged him to receive Master Philip as his personal legate. Alexander was eager to obtain detailed information about Prester John, the extent of his reputedly immense domain, and the nature of his faith. Philip's unenviable job was to find out the truth and report to his master.

Philip landed in the Near East, presumably in Palestine,

in order to proceed from there to the Prester's kingdom farther east. The ill-fated envoy probably lost his way in the desert and met with an untimely end, as nothing was ever heard of him again.

In spite of its failure, Philip's journey remains not only the first papal mission to the Far East, but also the earliest recorded attempt to open up relations between Christian Europe and the remote regions of Asia, a realm still shrouded in mystery. Alexander's embassy to Prester John, certainly one of the most curious episodes in the history of East-West contacts, can only be properly understood within the context of the European medieval conception of Asia and of contemporary political events. Now, Europe's vision of Asia in the twelfth century was itself a strange combination of Christian and pagan elements, some of them of considerable antiquity. The most significant body of tradition and, indeed, the foundation on which this whole conception rested, were the legends and myths inherited from the classical world.

CLASSICAL MARVELS

One of the most striking aspects of Europe's relations with East Asia is an almost total lack of cultural exchange until comparatively modern times in spite of trade contacts dating back to the pre-Christian era. Culture, as we now know, does not always follow commerce, particularly when the latter is carried out through various intermediaries, as was certainly the case of the Roman Empire and the countries of the remote Orient.

Take, for instance, silk which was probably the most popular luxury item in Rome in Augustus's day. Imported from China by Greek, Parthian, Syrian and Arab merchants, it was processed and dyed in Asia Minor to suit the Latin taste, and it was then shipped from Alexandria, Antioch and the other entrepôts of the eastern Mediterranean to the Roman markets. The proud owners of silk garments in Rome and elsewhere in Europe had only the vaguest notion about the origin of this precious commodity. Throughout antiquity people generally believed, Pausanias being the only notable exception, that the Seres, i.e. the Chinese, combed out the silk floss growing on the leaves of their tree, and that they traded it at a 'ghost market' near the border of their country, somewhere between India and Scythia. Indeed, even the great Virgil contributed to perpetuating the myth with his famous verses 'Need I tell you about . . . the way the Chinese comb the delicate silk from their leaves?' (*Georgics*, 118–21.)

According to a popular tradition, also current in the first century A.D., the Chinese were a just, frugal and peace-loving people, quite unlike the rowdy Romans. This idealized portrait, still currently accepted in the thirteenth century, owed its origin not to travellers' reports, but to the all too common belief that people of whom we know little or nothing have all the virtues we lack. It is, therefore, not surprising that the ancient Chinese too should have conceived the people of the remote West as the fortunate inhabitants of a rich, peaceful and wisely ruled empire, a fact repeatedly stressed in their early and medieval sources.

India, a country closer to Europe than China and one from which came a greater variety of products, was better known chiefly because of its early historical associations with Alexander the Great and his Bactrian Greek successors. However, before Alexander's campaign in 326 B.C., India already had a reputation in the Greek world as a land inhabited by fabulous beasts and most extraordinary people. Tales of wonder about India were related by nearly all the historians and geographers of classical antiquity, including Herodotus, and they were popularized in the Latin world by influential writers like Pliny, Ammianus Marcellinus and Arrian. These tales clearly originated from the distorted and magnified reports of sailors and traders: many a tall story must have been told by the Asiatic merchant to enhance the value of his exotic wares! The fact that these stories found their way into the works of reputable authors accounts for the well-established tradition of Marvels of the East, centred on India, which was uncritically accepted in Europe until the time of Marco Polo.

Thus for the Roman citizen under Trajan, as well as for the subjects of Henry III, India was not merely the distant land of pearls, precious stones, aromatic wood and spices, but also the home of men with a dog's head (Cynocephali), or a single foot (Monopodes), or with heels in front and the instep and toes turned backwards (Antipodes). It was the country of headless people with faces between the shoulders, of wild men without mouths who lived on the smell of flesh, fruit and flowers, of horned pigmies, of Hyperboreans who lived a thousand years, of Amazons and Satyrs, Brahmans and Gymnosophists, magic mountains and trees, of unicorns, griffins and gold-digging ants. These monsters and fabulous creatures haunted popular imagination throughout the Middle Ages and played a major role in both literature and art. We can still admire them today, carved in stone, on many a Gothic church.

As distance is an essential ingredient in the creation of myths and men are not so different at whatever latitude they live, we should not be surprised to find the same phenomenon, but in reverse, occurring in the Far East. In China, the country on the Asiatic continent farthest removed from Europe, there existed since the classical age of Han (II c.

22

B.C.–II c. A.D.) a special body of literature devoted to geographical lore. The most famous work of this kind is the *Shan hai ching* or *Classic of Mountains and Seas*. If we turn to the sections of this book which describe the inhabitants of the 'Western Regions' and of other remote countries, we find listed most of the weird creatures that the Mediterranean people had placed in the eastern part of the world, including the Cynocephali, the Monopodes and the headless people with their face in the breast. In China we also find the exact counterpart of the Latin myth of silk. The ancient Chinese believed that cotton, which they imported from Western Asia, was made of hair combed from certain 'water sheep'.

It is true that in the West a few less imaginative writers of antiquity, such as Strabo and Aulus Gellius, did not shrink from casting doubts on the traditional reports. Moreover, together with the fanciful tales, there existed also a less conspicuous body of scientific or quasi-scientific information, mainly of a geographical nature, on India and the sea and land routes to Asia. I refer to works like the *Periplus of the Erythrean Sea* (I c. A.D.) and Ptolemy's famous *Geography* (II c. A.D.). The anonymous Greek author of the *Periplus* not only gives a good account of Roman trade with India, but he also supplies a fairly accurate description of India's coast and markets, and of the maritime trade routes between India and the Mediterranean. A century later Ptolemy, on the basis of traders' reports, gave a detailed, although at times puzzling, description of the so-called Silk Route, i.e. the caravan route linking China with Mesopotamia. However, modern scholars have queried the genuine antiquity of this work in its present form.

Unfortunately, with the decline of Greek studies in the Latin West after the fifth century, the scientific contributions of the Hellenistic geographers were soon forgotten. Strabo's sober appraisal of traditional accounts about Asia was like-wise ignored. Pliny, Arrian and, in particular, Solinus (III c. A.D.) became the main source of knowledge about the East. The works of these authors combine fictional elements with geographical information in part derived from the Greek authors but otherwise largely mythological. Solinus, the principal representative of this 'erudite' tradition of marvels, had a tremendous influence, and his *Collection of Memorable Things*, a true storehouse of marvels, served as model for the later medieval encyclopaedists and cosmographers.

At the height of the empire, Roman power and influence never went much beyond the Caspian Sea and the fertile valleys of the Euphrates. Farther east lay vast and inhospit-able lands, endless plains, treacherous sands and immense mountain complexes. The populations of Western and Central Asia, such as the Parthians, Sogdians and Tokharians, often at odds with each other and their neighbours, were also constantly harassed by nomadic tribes of Turco-Mongolian stock from Siberia and Mongolia. Throughout the centuries empires rose and fell in the heart of Asia, yet news of these events seldom reached Europe. The Roman governors of the eastern provinces were far more concerned with local admin-istration and with the accumulation of private fortunes than with affairs beyond their borders. The disastrous defeat of Marcus Licinius Crassus at Carrhae in 53 B.C. had put an end to Rome's ambition to emulate Alexander. Besides, whatever happened in the heart of Asia, trade was seldom affected, and silk, furs and all the other exotic goods from the eastern lands continued to pour into the Roman markets.

At times Rome may have exerted some form of indirect control of trade with Asia by playing off one middleman against another and by imposing restrictions on luxury items at home, but at no time did she actually pose a direct challenge to the Middle Eastern merchants. Recorded cases of Roman missions to India and China, which certainly involved trade, are so few as to practically exclude any real aim, or ability, to compete with traders from Syria and the Arabian peninsula. Whatever control Rome may have had on the spice trade along the southern sea routes was lost in the third century when the Abyssinian kingdom of Axum extended its power over the Red Sea.

There is one recorded attempt of the Chinese to establish direct contact with the Roman empire. The envoy Kan Ying was despatched to the West in A.D. 97. Reaching the Persian Gulf he was about to embark on a ship bound for the Roman Orient when he was warned by his Parthian hosts that the voyage could take up to two years. He was also told that there was something in the sea that made people homesick, and that many had died of it. Kan Ying then gave up his attempt.

In the fifth century the Byzantine state established a monopoly of commerce in spices and silk within the Mediterranean world. However, soon afterwards the silk trade suffered a severe blow when silkworm eggs were smuggled out to the West by Nestorian monks and Byzantium began producing its own silk.

With the expansion of Moslem power in the seventh and eighth centuries, both the maritime and land routes across Central Asia fell under the control of the Arabs and, subsequently, the Turks. With a powerful Islam interposed between the now Christian West and Asia, Europe's isolation from the Eastern world became even greater, although spices and other luxuries continued to be bought at an increasingly higher price from the Arab middlemen. No significant information on the countries of East Asia from the

25

Arabs' rich geographical literature seems to have reached the West. The last two authors to write with some authority on India, Ceylon and China before the thirteenth century were the Greeks Cosmas Indicopleustes (*c.* 540) and Theophylactus Simocatta (*c.* 630). Their descriptions—in the case of Cosmas based in part on personal experience—had hardly any impact on Europe.

CHRISTIAN LEGENDS AND THE MEDIEVAL ALEXANDER

The lack of direct geographical knowledge and the spread of Christianity were largely responsible for the widespread acceptance in the early Middle Ages of a vision of the East coloured by all the traditional fabulous elements. The strange races and mythical animals described by classical authors found their rightful place within the Christian conception of the world which was then being elaborated by the Fathers of the Church and the apologetic writers. As the Bible was now the chief authority on all subjects, the origin of the fabulous races of men inhabiting the Eastern lands also had to be traced back to Adam. St. Augustine made this point quite clearly in his *City of God*, when he said that these monsters may have been created by the Almighty so that we should not wonder when freaks are born from us and blame Him for lack of wisdom. The pagan monsters were thus accepted as 'natural beings' and an integral part of God's creation.

A new tradition evolved in which, on the authority of Scripture and under the influence of both popular and erudite mythology, India and the inhabitants of Asia in general became at first identified with biblical localities and people, such as the Terrestrial Paradise and Gog and Magog, and then progressively 'christianized'.

The former development was partly responsible for the

perpetuation of old geographical errors, like that which made India an extension of Africa. This mistaken conception allowed in fact for a common source in Paradise of the four biblical rivers, one of which, the Geon or Gihon of the Septuagint, was for a long time identified with both the Oxus and the Nile, and another, the Pison, with both the Indus and the Ganges. In medieval cartography the so-called Three Indies, i.e. Greater, Lesser and Middle India, the latter inclusive of Ethiopia, occupy most of Asia. Farther to the west and behind Alexander's 'Iron Gate' (the Derbent Pass in the Caucasus) were relegated the foul people of Gog and Magog which, according to the Bible, Satan will one day set free to bring about the destruction of Jerusalem. The Holy City itself is placed in the centre of the inhabited world which in the maps is represented as an island surrounded by the Ocean (Mare Magnum).

The 'christianization' of Asia had also far-reaching consequences. It originated from the diffusion in the West of the legend of the Magi and the semi-legendary account of St. Thomas's mission to India, and found confirmation in the vague and distorted reports reaching Europe of the Nestorian activity in Central Asia, China and Mongolia, a topic to which we shall have to return presently.

St. Matthew's account of the Magi has always been one of the most popular episodes in the Gospel and since very early times it was enriched by the Church as well as by popular tradition with symbolic and allegorical elements. Thus it happened that the Wise Men from the East were invested with the dignity of kings without the flimsiest scriptural authority. The reinterpretation of this legend led to the widespread belief in the existence of Christian priest-kings ruling in the Orient.

The tradition of St. Thomas's apostolate in India goes back

27

to the apocryphal *Acts of Judas-Thomas* (?II–III c. A.D.), according to which St. Thomas preached the Gospel at the court of a Parthian prince of the Indus Valley. A later, popular tradition makes the Apostle preach among the Dravidian populations of the south. This southern tradition is the one held by the so-called Thomas Christians of the Syro-Malabar Church which traces its origin from St. Thomas's evangelization. However, the relation between the already doubtful mission of St. Thomas and the establishment of an early Christian community on the Coromandel coast, whose existence is mentioned for the first time in the sixth century by Cosmas Indicopleustes, is still open to question. Nevertheless, the tradition gained great popularity in the ninth century when King Alfred the Great actually sent an embassy to India with votive gifts for the tomb of St. Thomas, then reputed to be in Ceylon (A.D. 883). By this time the legend of the Magi and the account of St. Thomas's mission had been linked in a popular version of the story which made the Apostle go to the country of the Magi, baptize them and take them as his helpers.

Besides the Christian and biblical elements grafted on the erudite medieval conception of the Marvels of the East, the idealized picture of the remote lands of the Orient was constantly enriched by legends of a popular and romantic character that had been growing over the centuries around the figure of Alexander the Great. Semi-fictional accounts of the Macedonian king's exploits in India had early developed into colourful legends which were greatly influenced by the lore and taste of the Greek colonies of Asia Minor. These stories grew and spread in the Near East, and in the second and first centuries B.C. found literary expression in a series of imaginary *Letters*, the most famous of which was the *Letter of Alexander to Aristotle*. In it Alexander describes the wonders of

28

India to his teacher with such a wealth of detail as would satisfy the most demanding audience. India is portrayed as a fabled land inhabited by wild creatures and people, and the realm *par excellence* of magic and portents.

In the fourth century of our era the contents of these spurious letters, and of other equally fantastic reports, were used by an imaginative but, unfortunately, anonymous writer (almost certainly a Greco-Egyptian from Alexandria) to compile the first Alexander Romance.

This work was for a long time attributed to Aristotle's nephew Callisthenes, hence its title of *Pseudo-Callisthenes* by which it is usually known. Almost immediately translated into Latin by one Julius Valerius it gained immense popularity, and in the following centuries translations and versions appeared in almost every language. These often incorporated additional material drawn from the works of classical authors. A new and important translation in Latin was made by the Archpriest Leo (*c.* 950) of Naples which circulated under the title of *Historia de Proeliis* (*History of the Battles*). Leo's translation revived interest for the Alexander Saga, episodes from which, recited by itinerant minstrels in the streets and courts of Europe, gradually developed into full-length heroic poems such as the famous twelfth-century *Roman d'Alexandre*, and the equally famous Middle English metrical romance *King Alisaunder*. The character of the hero changed too in the process, and in the *Roman* he already impersonates the ideal courtly prince.

THE ORIGIN OF PRESTER JOHN

With Alexander entering and dominating the sphere of chivalry and courtly love, his legendary exploits in India and, indeed, the whole conception of Asia in the later Middle Ages

,ame tinged with chivalrous elements. While retaining its
,oulous pagan content as the habitat of weird animals and
,eople, Asia was also imagined as a land ruled by noble
kings living in great splendour and performing deeds worthy
of a Christian ruler. It was within this romantic and literary
context that in the middle of the twelfth century was born the
legend of Prester John.

The Magi and St. Thomas traditions, and the known existence of a Christian community in India, which at the time
was synonymous with the whole of farther Asia, provided an
ideal background for the widespread acceptance of this new
legend. Moreover, several real and imaginary factors added
credence to it, thus creating a psychological climate which
profoundly influenced the course of events in the following
century.

This extraordinary story begins with a visit to Rome in
May 1122 of an Eastern prelate named John. Who this prelate really was we do not know. He himself claimed to come
from India, and it was assumed for a long time that he was a
cleric from the Christian community on the Malabar coast
which after the Council of Ephesus in A.D. 431 had passed
under Nestorian jurisdiction. He certainly lectured on India
to the Roman Curia and caused a sensation throughout Italy
with his description of the miracles that occurred every year
in India on the feast of St. Thomas. He related how on that
day the perfectly preserved body of the Apostle would become animate, and with his arm administer Communion to
the faithful. As the tradition of this posthumous miracle is
not attested in any other independent source, whether
Western or Eastern, we may assume that John was either a
Nestorian from the Near East travelling under false pretences,
or, as is more likely, an outright impostor. Whatever the case,
about twenty years later, when the memory of his visit still

lingered, the news spread in Europe that a powerful Christian ruler of the East, called Prester John, had inflicted severe defeats on the Moslems. This report came from the Levant simultaneously with the tragic news of the fall of Edessa (the present Urfa in Turkey) and the massacre of the Frankish Crusaders by the troops of the Turkish atabeg Zengi (December 1144).

The German chronicler Otto of Freising (*d.* 1158) relates that the Bishop of Gabala in Syria, who brought this news to Pope Eugenius III in 1145, also told the pontiff how, a few years earlier, an Asiatic priest-king of Christian-Nestorian faith, called Prester John, had successfully fought the Persians. Apparently Prester John wanted to come to the assistance of the Crusaders in Jerusalem, but had been held up on the Tigris and had eventually returned home. The Bishop added that Prester John was reputed to be a descendant of the Magi and that he had been prompted to go to Jerusalem by the example of his illustrious ancestors.

The truth behind this account, which is the first reference to Prester John in the West, is still a matter of speculation. All we can say is that it must have grown out of confused reports, probably originating from the Nestorian communities of Persia and Mesopotamia, about the war waged against the Moslem rulers of Iran and Central Asia by Yeh-lü Ta-shih, founder of the Qara-Khitai empire. Yeh-lü Ta-shih was a prince of the Khitan, a people closely related to the Mongols, whose ancestors in the tenth century had conquered north China founding a kingdom which lasted until the twelfth century. Owing to the long period of Khitan rule, north China was known to many people in Asia as the land of Khitan or Khitai—hence the 'Cathay' of Marco Polo—and to this day Russians and Mongols designate China by variant forms of this name.

The Khitan dynasty, known in Chinese as Liao, was over-thrown in 1125 by the semi-nomadic Jurchen tribesmen from Manchuria who established a new dynasty in north China called the Chin or Golden dynasty. Yeh-lü Ta-shih with a large body of followers fled to Mongolia and thence to Central Asia. There he deposed a local Turkish ruler and in a few years he gained control of most of present-day Semirechye and Sinkiang where he founded a new state called Qara ('Black')-Khitai. He then began expanding westwards, and between 1137 and 1141 he conquered Bokhara and Samarkand, defeating in quick succession the Shah of Khorezm and the Seljuk sultan of Persia, Sanjar. At the time of his death in 1143, his empire extended from the Aral Sea in the west to Dzungaria and the Tarim in the east, and was undoubtedly one of the largest ever created in Central Asia. Ta-shih had early assumed the title of *gür-khan*, or Universal Ruler, which was also borne by all his successors to the Qara-Khitai throne.

Although Yeh-lü Ta-shih's religious beliefs are not very clear—some make him a Buddhist, others a Manichean—the Turkish and Iranian people over whom he and his descendants ruled for about eighty years comprised also many Nestorian Christians.

It may be recalled that Nestorius (*d.* A.D. 451), the Greek Patriarch of Constantinople, had been deposed by the Council of Ephesus, which had also condemned his doctrine as heretical. Nestorius had maintained that there are two distinct, yet closely united, natures in Christ, the human and the divine, and had refused to call Mary the God Bearer. Besides the purely theological issues, political considerations and personal antagonism unfortunately played a not insignificant part in the Council's hasty judgement. (Modern scholars have done much towards a full re-appraisal of Nestorius on

1. Fabulous beings. (a) (*above*) Headless Indians, from *Codex* 2810 of the Bibliothèque Nationale. Early fifteenth century. (b) (*below*) Headless Westerner, from the Chinese *Classic of Mountains and Seas*.

天臍口
雖化不服
乳目仍揮干戚

形天 無首操干戚而舞以
乳為目以臍為口
爭神 不勝為帝所戮遂
厥形

2. Sketch of a Mongol archer by Antonio Pisanello, *c.* 1440.

the basis of newly discovered documents.) His followers preached the dyophysite teaching first at Edessa, then at Nisibis in Persia. The Persian rulers of the Sassanid dynasty (224–632) supported the Catholicos, or Patriarch, of the Nestorians who resided at Seleucia on the Tigris because he was traditionally opposed to Rome. As a result, the Nestorians were able to carry out an intense missionary activity that for several centuries was unrivalled by any other Christian Church. They penetrated into West Turkestan as early as the sixth century, and between the seventh and eighth centuries Nestorian communities were established in various parts of East Turkestan and as far as China. At the beginning of the eleventh century Nestorianism had followers even among the nomadic tribes of Mongolia. In spite of occasional brutal persecutions and the constant challenge of other faiths, such as Buddhism and Manicheism (the syncretic religion founded in the third century by the prophet Mani of Babylon), Nestorianism flourished in Asia until the fourteenth century reaching through caravan and sea routes the remotest corners of the continent. The tremendous expansion of this religion in Asia was due chiefly to the zeal and learning of the Syrian missionaries, but owed much also to its early association with commercial interests.

Now, the important Nestorian communities of Syria and Asia Minor in the eleventh and twelfth centuries were kept informed of the situation in distant parts of the Orient through trade and their ecclesiastical network. Some of this information occasionally filtered into the West from Byzantium and the Frankish *Outremer*. The news of Yeh-lü Ta-shih's victory over Sanjar in 1141 divulged by the Nestorians (who may have also claimed Ta-shih as one of their converts) and the knowledge of the existence of Christians in the remote East seem to have given origin to the myth of Prester

John. His priestly and royal attributes are simply those that the Christian legend had since early times conferred on the Wise Men of the Bible. His name is more puzzling. It has been suggested that John, in Syriac 'Yuhunan', may represent a phonetic approximation, admittedly very faint, of the title 'gür-khan'. On the other hand John was not only one of the most common Nestorian names, but was also one found in the early legends of the St. Thomas cycle. The false Indian prelate, whose sensational visit to Rome in 1122 has been described earlier, was likewise called John. In other words John, because of its many religious and historical connotations, was an ideal name for the Eastern priest-king, and this may perhaps explain why it was chosen in the first place.

PRESTER JOHN, KING DAVID AND THE CRUSADES

Whatever the origin, still debatable, of the myth and the name, we know that the truth of the Bishop of Gabala's report was not questioned. Also no doubts were cast on the Christian faith of Prester John, for it was implicitly assumed that all those who fought Islam must be Christian. Moreover, at the time when the news of the fall of Edessa had shocked and disheartened Europe, the story of Prester John offered fresh hopes for the crusading movement.

These still vague expectations received a powerful boost twenty years later, when the Second Crusade, launched by Pope Eugenius III and the King of France, had already failed in its objectives because of the perennial discord and jealousy that plagued the Christian camp. Sometime in 1165 a letter purporting to come from Prester John began circulating in Europe. This strange missive was originally addressed to the Byzantine emperor Manuel I Comnenus

(1143–80), but according to later accounts it was also directed to the pope, the Holy Roman Emperor Frederick I Barbarossa, and other European monarchs.

In his letter Prester John claims to rule over the Three Indies, a territory which he explains extends from the Tower of Babel to the place where the sun rises. After having announced his intention of defeating the enemies of Christ and of visiting the Holy Sepulchre, Prester John enumerates his treasures and the marvels of his kingdom. This is an impressive catalogue of all the wonders traditionally located in India, including the tomb of St. Thomas.

The letter of the wise ruler of the East was, of course, a fabrication, but to this day and in spite of much meticulous research its real author is still unknown. He was undoubtedly a man well versed in religious and profane literature, as shown by his detailed description of Asia, largely inspired by the famous *Letter of Alexander*. Some scholars have suggested that he may have been a high-ranking cleric profoundly disturbed by the bitter conflict between Church and Empire which had just begun to afflict the Christian world. In sharp contrast to the disruptive situation arising in Europe as a result of this struggle, Prester John's letter offers the example of a theocratic sovereign combining in one the virtues of king and high priest, and ruling peacefully and justly over innumerable people and immense territory. This utopian picture, in which were admirably fused all the colourful aspects of Asia dear to popular imagination, may have been designed to impress upon pope and lay rulers of Europe the futility and pettiness of their quarrels. On the other hand it seems, from internal evidence, that like the author of the *Pseudo-Callisthenes*, the anonymous forger of the letter had spent some time in the Near East, possibly in *Outremer*. It is more likely, then, that the letter was composed with the definite aim of strengthening the current rumours about the existence of the powerful Eastern monarch, and of fostering hopes of his intervention on the side of the crusading nations.

This strange document, whose authenticity was likewise unquestioned until centuries later, gained wide circulation and immense popularity, as can be seen from the great number of manuscript copies that have come down to us. It so impressed the papal court that, after Alexander III with the help of the Lombard League had defeated Barbarossa in 1176, it was decided to send a special envoy to Prester John with the pope's belated reply. The choice fell on Philip, the pope's own physician, whose misadventure has already been related.

The failure of the papal mission in no way affected the now well-established belief in the mythical sovereign of the Indies. On the contrary, the pontiff's much publicized reply did much to kindle the hope, cherished by the Crusaders, of finding in him the powerful ally who would help them crush once and for all the heathen Saracens.

In the last two decades of the twelfth century the situation in the Frankish *Outremer* had steadily deteriorated. The successful campaigns of Zengi's son Nur al-Din (*d.* 1173) against the Latins, followed by the reoccupation of Palestine by the great Salah al-Din, better known in the West as Saladin (*d.* 1193), had practically wiped out the substantial achievements of the First Crusade. By 1190 the Franks had lost Jerusalem, captured three years earlier by Saladin, as well as much of the coast and all the hinterland.

The Third Crusade (1189–92), led by King Richard I 'Cœur de Lion', established the new Latin kingdom of Cyprus, but failed to recover Jerusalem, again because of political dissensions among the Christian leaders. As for the Fourth Crusade, its diversion to the Byzantine empire ended with the tragic sack of Constantinople (1204), rightly described by Sir Steven Runciman as one of the greatest crimes in history, and one for which Venetian cupidity must bear much of the blame.

A lull followed of which the new, energetic pope Innocent III (1198–1216) took advantage to strengthen the authority of the Church in Europe. Heresies were spreading across the length and breadth of the continent, some stemming from Gnostic roots, like the dualist 'neo-Manichean' doctrine of the Cathari, others from even deeper and more obscure origins. The ferocious Albigensian Crusade (1209), directed against the Cathari of southern France, inaugurated Christian Europe's holy war on heresy, a war which was to be pursued relentlessly by the Church for the next three hundred years through the instrument of the Inquisition.

However, Innocent's dream was to reconquer Jerusalem. The ill-fated Children's Crusade of 1212—the echo of which still lingers today in the legend of the Pied Piper of Hamelin—prompted the pope to renew his efforts in this direction. These led to the Lateran Council of 1215 and the proclamation of the Fifth Crusade. The Crusade was to start two years later with the participation of all European monarchs, but Innocent's death in 1216 upset the whole project. His successor, the aged Honorius III (1216–27), had great difficulties in rallying the kings to the Cross. After several setbacks the Christian army which was composed mainly of Austrian, Hungarian and Dutch Crusaders, and later joined by French and English contingents, eventually reached Palestine in 1218.

In the meantime the Bishop of Acre, James of Vitry, had been carrying out a vigorous propaganda for the Crusade among the Latin settlers in the Levant. It is in one of the bishop's letters, written in 1217, that we again meet with

37

Prester John. He is mentioned together with the 'many Christian kings living in the Orient' who had heard of the advent of the Crusaders and were about to come to their help in the war against the Saracens. This and similar allusions roused a mood of fervent expectation among the Christian troops which later events proved to be deceptive.

As their first objective, the Crusaders planned an attack on Egypt, then ruled by the elderly Ayyubid sultan Saif al-Din, known in the West as Saphadin. Accordingly they laid siege to Damietta, the key port on the eastern delta of the Nile. The siege lasted more than a year and ended with the capitulation of the city in November 1219.

Besides its importance in the military history of the Crusades, the attack on Damietta is notable also for two events. These, although quite unrelated, will be of great significance in the future contacts between Christendom and the Orient.

The first is the presence in the Christian camp of Francis of Assisi (1182–1226). The Italian friar had joined the Crusade in the hope of converting the sultan and thus peacefully regaining the Holy Land. He was the first among the founders of Western religious orders to impose on his followers the duty to carry out the conversion of heathens in distant regions through preaching and example. Francis himself had earlier tried to go to Syria (1212) and Morocco (1213?) to evangelize, but ill-health and unfavourable winds prevented him from carrying out his task. In May 1217, at the First General Chapter of the Friars Minor gathered in Assisi, the overseas Province of Terra Santa (Holy Land) was established and Brother Elias was appointed as its first Minister.

St. Francis's well-known attempt to convert Saphadin's son and successor al-Kamil in 1219 was not successful, but his journey to Syria and his presence in Egypt consecrated, as it were, the newly born Franciscan missionary movement in the East. It also made his friars the most eligible candidates for the delicate diplomatic and apostolic work of the Church in Mongolia and China in the thirteenth and fourteenth centuries.

The other notable event concerns the diffusion among the Crusaders, immediately before and after the fall of Damietta, of documents containing various prophecies of victory for the Christian forces, including the forthcoming conquest of Jerusalem. One of these prophecies mentioned also the intervention of the king of Abyssinia on the side of the Christians, and his capture of Mecca.

Another apocryphal document which apparently reached the Christians in rather mysterious circumstances at the beginning of 1221 was the so-called *Report on King David*. This curious document described the victorious advance into Persia of 'King David, Christian King of India, sent by the Lord to crush the heathen and destroy Mahomet's teaching'. There are several contemporary versions of the *Report*. In some of them King David is identified with Prester John, in others he appears as his son or grandson.

The *Report* was received with great jubilation at Damietta, as it added strength to the prophecies and confirmed those rumours about the imminent arrival of Prester John that had been circulating for some time. Here, again, no one seems to have suspected a forgery. James of Vitry quoted amply from the document in a letter to Pope Honorius. Encouraged by all these favourable omens, the pope's representative at the Crusade, the Spanish Cardinal Pelagius, refused the sultan's offers of peace and decided to march on Cairo to inflict what he now firmly believed would be the death-blow to Islam.

Alas, the prophecies did not come true. The Negus of Abyssinia and King David failed to materialize and the march on Cairo ended in utter disaster for the Christian forces, in the loss of Damietta and the collapse of the Crusade (July–September 1221).

As with the earlier *Letter of Prester John*, the real author or authors of the Damietta prophecies are not known. However, from internal evidence it seems certain that these documents proceeded, as most of the rumours on Prester John, from the Nestorian communities in Syria, and that these in turn had enlarged upon reports received from the Nestorian sources in Central Asia.

The Nestorian circles in the Middle East that forged the *Report on King David* in all probability merely wished to impress the Moslem princes of Syria and Egypt and make them less hostile towards the eastern Christian communities. Similar reports had also been circulating in Armenia. Whatever their original purpose, they were unquestionably used by the leaders of the Crusade as effective means to overcome adverse criticism and lack of co-operation in the Christian camp, and to urge a definite course of action. We shall probably never know the extent to which the Spanish cardinal, the fiery Bishop of Acre, or the Knights Templars were involved in the manipulation of these prophetic documents to further their aims, but we are now in a position to identify the real historical figure that gave origin to the legend of King David. However, in order to do this, we must look into what happened in Asia in the early part of the thirteenth century.

II

The Mongols and Europe

FRIAR JULIAN'S REPORT: FACTS AND FICTION ABOUT
THE MONGOLS

Judging at least by its consequences, the most important
event in Asia at the beginning of the thirteenth century was
the rise of the Mongols to world power. Their impact, as we
all know, was dramatically felt also in the West but, strangely
enough, the European nations, including those that bore the
brunt of the Mongol invasion, were for a long time in almost
total darkness as to the true nature of the nomadic conquerors
and the origin of their power.

One of the most interesting documents on the Mongols
before the first-hand reports of the Franciscans John of Pian
di Carpine and William of Rubruck is the relation of Julian,
a Dominican friar from Hungary, who as emissary of King
Béla IV journeyed to the Volga–Ural region in 1234–35 and
to east Russia in 1237.

In the course of these exploratory missions and, in particular, during his last journey, which was actually interrup-
ted by the Mongols' attack on the Russian principalities, the
brave Dominican was able to collect much information on
these awesome warriors. His report, about which we shall
have more to say later on, is especially valuable to us in so far
as it contains, together with accurate data, also a good deal
of fictional material on the rise of the Mongols.

According to Friar Julian, the Mongol conquest originated from a contest between one of their chiefs and the sister of another chieftain, who in the end was seduced by him and killed. The friar's account is a version of a story, then already popular in Central and Western Asia. Its main theme was Chingis Khan's request of a powerful chieftain's daughter as bride and the war ensuing from the father's refusal to comply. This story, which was picked up also by other Western travellers in Asia including Marco Polo, is in turn related (as we shall see) to a particular development of the Prester John legend.

In Julian's report we find also a colourful description of the wealth and splendour of the Mongol court, including such marvels as the Great Khan's palaces with golden pillars and gates, obviously inspired by the European literary image of the Orient with which the learned Dominican was familiar. At the same time, Julian's observations on the expansionist programme of the Mongols, their war tactics based on mobility, and their strategy in conquering fortified towns, are very accurate, and in this respect his account may be regarded as a forerunner of the Franciscan reports.

The peculiar blend of fact and fiction which characterizes the early European views of the Mongols shows the influence of the legend grown around the figure of Chingis Khan, the man who was responsible for the unification of the Mongolian tribes and for their swift conquest of much of continental Asia and eastern Europe.

Chingis Khan's amazing career has left an indelible mark on world history and literature; however, it is only in comparatively recent times that the true facts of his life have been firmly established. As our story is directly related to the Mongol conquest, we must now turn to these facts and see how they affected the course of history in the West.

MONGOL TRIBES AND THE RISE OF CHINGIS KHAN

The life of Chingis Khan can be, and has in fact been, reconstructed mainly on the basis of Mongolian, Persian and Chinese sources. The most important document is an imperial chronicle in Mongolian, consisting largely of a biography of Chingis Khan, which was discovered in China about a hundred years ago. Known as the *Secret History of the Mongols* because it was kept in the secret archives of the Mongol court, this document is not only an extremely rich mine of information on Chingis Khan, his family and the Mongol tribes, but it is also a literary work of great merit. Indeed, as Arthur Waley has pointed out, portions of it are among the most vivid primitive literature that exists anywhere in the world. The part dealing with the life of Chingis Khan was composed in Mongolia in 1228, just one year after the death of the conqueror.

Written partly in alliterative verse, the *Secret History* has a saga-like quality, especially in the description of heroic and dramatic scenes. There is, indeed, drama on every page. The gory details may often shock the sensitive reader, but they provide us with a direct insight into the life of the medieval Mongols. Rape and plunder were as natural to them as horse-breeding, sheep-herding and moving with their flocks and felt tents from place to place. This was due to geographic and economic factors, and also to a nomadic sociocultural tradition evolved within the tribes over the ages which permeated, as it were, all aspects of their life. While the economy of the steppe governed their migrations and accounted for much of their 'plundering urge' against settled civilizations, their extended patrilinear system of blood relations governed marriages and alliances, and was in turn the source of endless feuds and fratricidal wars. Now, these

43

wars had been going on for centuries among the Turco-Mongolian, i.e. Turkish-speaking and Mongol-speaking, tribes of Inner Asia. Every now and then an energetic and lucky chieftain would succeed in unifying the tribes and create a confederacy of steppe people, a sort of nomadic empire like that of the Hsiung-nu (II c. B.C.–I c. A.D.), the Juan-juan (V–VI c. A.D.), the T'u-chüeh (VI–VIII c. A.D.) and the Uighurs (VIII–IX c. A.D.).

Often, economic and social pressure within the confederacy, and the political weakness of the neighbouring civilizations in the south and the west, turned the nomadic horsemen's raids into a full-fledged war of conquest. If successful, the leader of the confederacy would found a kingdom in China, Central Asia or even eastern Europe and thus begin a 'barbarian dynasty'. In time this dynasty was assimilated, to a greater or lesser degree, by the higher civilization of the conquered country; the barbarian rulers became literate and civilized and, in the process, they inevitably estranged themselves from the steppe society and their own nomadic tradition. Eventually they were dispossessed by a new barbarian invader or by a nativist movement in their kingdom.

Chinese history is interspersed with such barbarian dynasties, some short-lived, some lasting centuries, like the last dynasty of all, the Ch'ing (1644–1911), founded by Manchu tribes. But usually the barbarian confederations were short-lived. Inherent tribal differences tended to come into the open early. Rival leaders then emerged and the tribal state would break up, reverting, by an inexorable process of fragmentation peculiar to nomadic societies, to a loose complex of separate and conflicting tribal units whose individual history is hard to trace and is, therefore, mostly unknown.

Thus, our knowledge of the Turco-Mongolian tribes living in that great steppe-world of the nomads that extends from south Russia to Manchuria, and which is sometimes referred to as Central Eurasia, is confined chiefly to those periods when the tribes enjoyed ephemeral unity and their power was felt by neighbouring nations.

Although the situation in Mongolia before Chingis Khan is obscure, we know that at the time of his birth, about 1167, most of the important tribes had their own territory, even if somewhat ill-defined, within which they moved according to the season.

The leading tribes were the Naiman in western Mongolia, towards the Altai mountains; the Merkit and Kereit in central Mongolia, south of the Baikal; the 'Mongol' proper and the Tatar farther east, the latter close to the Manchurian border. In the early twelfth century the Tatars were probably the most powerful people in Mongolia and had close relations with the Jurchen rulers of north China who supported them against the other tribes. This is why in China the people of Mongolia were cumulatively known as *Ta-ta*, or Tatars, and it is also by this name that they were known among all the Turkish, Arabic and Persian speaking peoples of Asia.

Some of these tribes were more civilized—perhaps it would be better to say less barbarian—than others in so far as they had been reached by Nestorian missionaries, or exposed to the cultural influence of the more advanced Turkish people of Central Asia, such as the Uighurs. The latter's kingdom, with its capital near present-day Turfan in Sinkiang, had been an important cultural centre since the ninth century, when the Uighurs had moved there from their original home in northern Mongolia after the collapse of their empire. Converted first to Manicheism and Buddhism, many

45

Uighur Turks had subsequently embraced Nestorian Christianity. Under the multiple influence of these religions and of Chinese culture they had developed a brilliant and highly cosmopolitan civilization which lasted well over three centuries, and which still speaks to us through the numerous manuscripts and artifacts that have survived. The Silk Route on which the Uighur state was situated brought them into contact with other cultural centres of Central and Western Asia, while their proximity to the Altai and the Gobi gave them an easy access also to the nomadic peoples of Mongolia.

The Naimans took on Turkish titles, the Nestorian faith and the Uighur alphabet (a script deriving from Aramaic through Sogdian). The Kereit tribe, or at least its ruling clan, had also been converted to Nestorianism probably from the beginning of the eleventh century, and its leaders bore Christian names. At the end of that century Nestorian missionaries from Central Asia had penetrated among the Tatars of eastern Mongolia, for we know that their chiefs too had Christian names like John and Mark. Christians were also found among the Merkits and in some of the other tribes. To be sure, Nestorianism added but a thin veneer of civilization, and it is doubtful whether any of the converted tribesmen ever abandoned their native shamanism with all its strange admixture of animistic beliefs, divination and sorcery. Nor, as far as one can judge, were their warlike customs greatly affected by Christianity. Perhaps it would be more correct to say that they borrowed from other cultures only those elements that had an obviously practical or prestige value. The adoption of Christianity was seemingly conceived by their leaders as a means of obtaining the assistance of yet another superhuman power, and this was in no way incompatible with their traditional beliefs.

These beliefs revolved around the hazy notion of an all-powerful Tengri (pronounced Tenggeri) or Heaven, which the Turkish and Mongolian nomads of Inner Asia had worshipped as their sky-god and supreme deity since antiquity. Its counterpart was Itügen, the popular goddess of earth and fertility. These two deities as well as the sun and the moon, the forces of nature, the spirits of sacred mountains and rivers, and the souls of the tribal chiefs and of ancestors were worshipped and propitiated with obeisance and offerings of food and drink, often involving also human and animal sacrifices. The Mongols made idols of felt and other stuff and believed that the spirits dwelt in them. They were kept inside the yurt as tutelary gods, or placed outside in special carts for general worship. Special precautions had to be taken to avoid defiling the earth and the water, hence their complicated system of taboos, purification ritual, usually by fire, and elaborate burial rules.

The clan into which Chingis Khan was born belonged to the 'Mongol' tribe of north-eastern Mongolia—broadly the region crossed by the Onon and Kerulen rivers—which does not seem to have been touched either by Uighur culture or by Christianity. His ancestors had been tribal leaders for several generations, but the family fortunes had declined and after the death of his father, poisoned by rival Tatar tribesmen, his mother and her children were abandoned by relatives and retainers and deprived of their inheritance.

When these events took place, Chingis Khan, then known simply as Temüjin (the name he had been given at birth), was only eight years old. The family, whose only property consisted of a herd of nine horses, led a miserable and precarious life for several years, constantly moving in search of food or fleeing from unfriendly tribesmen.

His mother Hö'elün, a strong and practical woman in the

best Mongolian tradition, bravely looked after the brood. This is how the *Secret History* portrays her in verse:

> *Pulling firmly her cap*
> *Over her head,*
> *Tying tightly her belt*
> *To shorten her skirt,*
> *Along the river Onon,*
> *Running up and down,*
> *She gathered wild apples and berries.*
> *Night and day she was filling*
> *Their hungry gullets.*

After various adventures, Temüjin eventually succeeded in obtaining the support of Toghril, the *Ong-khan* or king of the powerful Kereit tribe and former friend of his father. With Toghril's protection and the help of Jamuqa, a sworn brother from his infancy, Temüjin was able to dispose of his immediate enemies. Then he gradually conquered or rallied to him various smaller neighbouring tribes, his reputation growing with each victory.

His basic technique was very simple. He would create an alliance with a friendly tribe and jointly attack another tribe; subsequently, he would form a new alliance to destroy his former partner, who by now had become a dangerous rival. Both Toghril and Jamuqa, to whom he owed much of his success, perished at his hands. He was always careful, however, to give his actions a valid and morally acceptable justification, usually by turning the blame on his former allies and claiming himself to be the innocent victim of their intrigues.

Contrary to the generally accepted belief he was not a bloodthirsty savage. Whenever he resorted to cruelty, as he often did, it was not out of sheer sadism, but for a definite

3. Portraits of Mongol emperors. (a) (*above left*) Chingis Khan (1206–27).
(b) (*above right*) Ögödei (1229–41). (c) (*below left*) Kublai (1260–94). (d)
(*below right*) Temür Öljeitü (1294–1306). Artists unknown. Thirteenth to
fourteenth centuries.

4. Seals of the Mongol period. (a) (*above*) Seal of the Great Khan Güyüg (1246–48). Mongolian in Uighur script. (b) (*below*) Seal of the Nestorian Patriarch Mar Yahballaha III (1281–1317). Turkish in Syriac script.

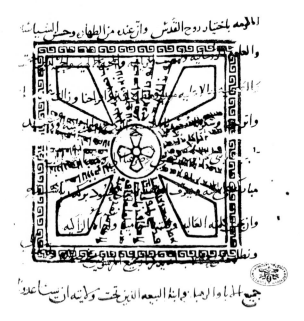

purpose, for instance to discourage resistance, and this fact alone places him above most of the tribal leaders of his time. He preferred cunning and diplomacy, but when he could not achieve his aims in this way he would fight coolly and only after careful preparation.

It was, essentially, his sober judgement and keen understanding of men and steppe society that enabled him to gather around him a group of trusted and utterly devoted followers, without whose help he would never have been able to rise to the top. Most of these early comrades (*nököd*) were warriors who had voluntarily relinquished their own tribes to join Temüjin. They formed an armed volunteer force similar to the medieval French *truste* and, as with the members of a *truste*, their relation to the leader was typically feudal in nature.

In 1202 Temüjin conquered and incorporated the Tatar tribe, a year later the Kereit, and in 1204 the same lot fell to the Naiman. On this occasion he also captured the secretary of the Naiman chief, an Uighur scribe, whom he took into his service. The adoption of the Uighur script by the Mongols dates traditionally from this year, but its use was confined chiefly to the rudimentary chancellery established in the following years to keep records of legal judgements and administrative matters.

The Naiman ruler perished in the onslaught but his young son Küchlüg ('the Strong') managed to escape. His adventurous flight from Mongolia, across the Altai and into Central Asia, was a repetition of Yeh-lü Ta-shih's feat eighty years before. With a small band of followers Küchlüg reached the Qara-Khitai kingdom. He married the daughter of the last gür-khan and before long he ousted him, assuming his title and power. It seems that under his wife's influence Küchlüg repudiated his Nestorian faith and embraced

Buddhism. At any rate he began to persecute the Moslems, forcing them to become either Christians or Buddhists. This policy and his territorial ambition soon brought him into conflict with his powerful western neighbour Muhammad-Shah, the Turkish sultan of Khorezm.

The echo of Küchlüg's activity against the Moslems in Central Asia reached the Crusaders' army in the Near East and it was responsible for the revival of the Prester John legend, with the ex-Christian Naiman prince now assuming the identity of David, King of the Indies and scourge of Islam. In the eyes of the Nestorians who circulated this story there was, clearly, a connection between King David, alias Küchlüg (incidentally, David may well have been Küchlüg's Christian name), and Prester John. Was not the former a successor, in name as well as in deed, of Yeh-lü Ta-shih, the original Prester John? Both ruled over the same kingdom with the title of gür-khan, both fought against the Moslems and both were, perhaps less justifiably, regarded as Christians. But no one can really blame the Nestorian propagandists for appropriating two kings to their faith, one of whom was certainly sympathetic to Christianity and the other a Christian by birth.

Two years after Küchlüg's flight, Temüjin was master of the whole of Mongolia. His sovereignty was formally consecrated by a pan-Mongolian diet held at the sources of the Onon. His old and faithful companions were rewarded with high ranks, grants of serfs, and special privileges. The tribal armies were integrated into a unified force, and an élite body of soldiers was set up to serve as the personal guard of the new leader and the backbone of the Mongol military machine. On this occasion Temüjin assumed the name of Chingis Khan by which he is usually known. This name is really a title which, like gür-khan, means 'universal ruler'.

CHINGIS'S CAMPAIGNS IN CHINA AND THE WEST

Chingis Khan was a mature man of forty when he began his career as world conqueror. Up to his election in 1206 it is doubtful whether he suffered from the 'Alexander complex'; however, after this date he seems to have developed a profound conviction that Heaven wished to submit the whole world to Mongol rule, and that he had been entrusted with this mission. Chingis's faith in his role as leader of men was strengthened by the pronouncements of the shaman Kökö-chü who, as the chief intermediary between men and the world of spirits, wielded great power among the Mongols. The part played by Kököchü in consecrating Chingis Khan as supreme chief 'appointed by Heaven to rule over mankind' was very significant, even though Chingis subsequently eliminated the shaman whose prestige posed a direct threat to his own authority.

Having removed all opposition in Mongolia Chingis Khan turned his attention to China, his immediate neighbour in the south and a rich country whose wealth had attracted all nomads since the beginning of history.

In the early fourteenth century China was divided into several kingdoms. Most of the northern provinces were ruled by the Jurchen who, as we have already seen, had founded the Chin or Golden dynasty. These uncouth and fierce semi-nomadic barbarians from the Manchurian woodland had assimilated Chinese culture even more rapidly than their Khitan predecessors, and by the turn of the century their ruling élite was thoroughly sinicized. Their capital was Chung-tu, which corresponds to modern Peking.

In northwest China, in the present-day provinces of Kansu and Ninghsia, there was the small state of Hsi-Hsia founded in the ninth century by Tibetans, whose culture was an

51

interesting mixture of Tibetan, Chinese and even Turkish elements. Some Uighur tribes had also settled in this country and the dominant religion was Buddhism.

In the southern half of China the national Sung dynasty ruled. The Sung capital was Hangchow, the richest and most magnificent city of the world, later immortalized in the West by Marco Polo's description. The Sung were then enjoying a life of great refinement and culture which some would regard as the apex of Chinese civilization.

The two foreign states in the north were in almost constant conflict with each other and with the Sung in spite of treaties settling boundaries and mutual relations. The Sung emperors had in the past tried unsuccessfully to repel the invaders, and in the end had been forced to accept humiliating conditions in the form of a heavy annual tribute to the Jurchen in order to maintain the uneasy *status quo.*

To complete the picture we must mention the Öngüt people who lived in the Ordos region near the great bend of the Yellow River north of the Great Wall. They were Turkish tribes that had been converted to Nestorianism for several generations. In 1204 the Öngüt ruler had pledged his support to Chingis Khan and this alliance was later sealed with the marriage of the ruler's son to a daughter of Chingis.

Chingis Khan's first move towards the conquest of north China was to obtain the submission of the Hsi-Hsia king, and having achieved this with a show of force in 1211 he attacked the Chin territory. Having ravaged the border region, his army laid siege to Peking which capitulated in 1215 after a long resistance. The plunder and fire lasted several weeks and much of the population was either killed or deported. The Mongols showed little mercy to towns that offered any resistance as they were not yet trained in siege techniques, and usually lost many men during a prolonged siege. So, when the town capitulated, most of the inhabitants were put to the sword; only selected women, children, skilled crafts-men and religious leaders were spared. The knowledge of the Mongols' ruthlessness towards the conquered people often acted as a deterrent. This was certainly the case in north China where many fortresses capitulated through the defec-tion of the garrison commanders, who were subsequently reinstated in their position by the Mongols.

While his generals carried on the war against the Jurchen, Chingis returned to the north. He had received, too, various reports about Küchlüg's activity in Turkestan, but they were more accurate than those received by the Crusaders at the other end of Asia. Küchlüg's rise to power was disturbing, and Chingis decided that he could no longer defer the destruction of his old foe. In 1218 he sent an expedition against the Qara-Khitai ruler. The Mongol troops invaded the king-dom, welcomed by the oppressed Moslem population, and soon after caught and slew Küchlüg. The conquest of Semi-rechye and Sinkiang brought the Mongols to the gates of the Khorezmian empire, which then extended over present Uzbekistan, Iran and Afghanistan. The sultan viewed this development with great concern, as the internal situation in his country was unstable and his own position somewhat in-secure. Fearing that Chingis would eventually invade his territory, Muhammad provoked a *casus belli* in 1219 by failing to pay the Mongols compensation for a trading caravan mas-sacred by the governor of Otrar (a frontier town on the Syr Darya), and by killing Chingis Khan's envoys. The execution of ambassadors, one of the gravest crimes in the eyes of the Mongols, was tantamount to a declaration of war.

The 'Otrar incident' is, like the contemporary siege of Damietta, a turning-point in history. It triggered off one of the most destructive invasions, as the Mongol horsemen's aim was not so much to conquer as to inflict punishment. Muhammad's forces, superior in number, but composed mainly of Turkish mercenaries and lacking cohesion, were annihilated. Most of the towns were destroyed and the civilian population massacred. Damage to the country was so great that entire provinces in southern Persia and Afghanistan never recovered. The rich and beautiful cities of Bukhara, Samarkand, Balkh, Nishapur, Merv and Herat were sacked and burnt; Gurganj, the capital of Khorezm on the Amu Darya, was flooded by damming the river. The Mongol onslaught was epitomized by an eye-witness of the capture of Bukhara as follows: 'They came, they sapped, they burnt, they slew, they plundered and they departed.'

The effete Muhammad, abandoned by his followers, died of disease and despair on an island off the eastern shores of the Caspian to which he had fled in 1220. His son Jalal al-Din who, unlike his father, was a brilliant warrior for whom even Chingis had admiration, fought valiantly against the invader, but was eventually defeated and saved his life by fleeing to India.

Jebe and Sübötei, the two generals whom Chingis Khan had sent in pursuit of the sultan, did not come back after they had learnt of his death. Under the command of Chingis's eldest son Jochi, and carried by their own momentum, they pushed westwards from Persia, and after sacking various cities south of the Caspian, invaded Georgia. Thence, across the Caucasus, they penetrated into the south Russian steppe.

This territory, the major thoroughfare between Europe and Asia and the classic route of invasion, was inhabited by people of Iranian and Turkish stock. Chief among them were the Alans or Ossets, Christian descendants of the ancient Sarmatians, the Lesgis or Lesgians, the Circassians, and the Kipchak Turks, also known as Comans and Polovchi.

The Mongols defeated these semi-sedentary populations in quick succession, and shortly after, on 31 May 1223, had their first serious engagement with the Russian forces that had come to the help of the Comans. It took place near the little river Kalka, now Kal'chik, north of the Sea of Azov. The 80,000 strong Russian army led by the Princes of Galicia and Kiev was cut to pieces. Mstislav, Prince of Kiev, resisted for three days in his camp, but was in the end forced to surrender and was later cruelly executed.

The Mongols' anger had again been roused to a pitch by the slaying of the two envoys whom they had sent earlier to negotiate with the Russian princes. However, they could not linger in Russia and had to turn back, but not without first plundering Soldaia (Sudak), the flourishing Genoese trading station on the southeastern coast of Crimea.

On their return journey the Mongols crossed the territory north of the Caspian and the Aral seas, then inhabited by the Volga Bulgars and the Kangli Turks, and in the spring of 1224 they rejoined Chingis Khan's main army on the Syr Darya.

This amazing feat and the success that followed most of the Mongols' campaigns were largely due to the military strategy and army organization introduced by Chingis Khan. Much information on the subject is found in the *Secret History*, as well as in many other contemporary Oriental and Western sources.

The Mongol army, which comprised all able-bodied men between the age of fifteen and seventy, was divided into units of ten, a hundred, a thousand and ten thousand men, the leader of each unit being under the orders of the leader of the unit immediately above him. Thus, a leader-of-a-hundred was responsible for the ten leaders-of-ten under him, and so on.

This pyramidal structure, at the top of which stood Chingis Khan and his generals, who were in command of several units of ten thousand men each, was held together by the strictest discipline and by a total devotion to the leaders. According to the draconian Mongol code of law (*Jasagh* or *Yasa*) drawn up by Chingis Khan, any breach of military discipline was usually punished with death. The same hierarchical order obtained, of course, in the distribution of booty after a successful campaign.

In the brief spells between wars both men and horses were kept fit and in constant training by means of massive seasonal hunts organized and led by the khan himself. Physical toughness was paramount: soldiers and their mounts were expected to cover great distances under the most trying weather conditions and with limited food supplies, and to be ready to fight against usually superior forces at the end of the journey. For this reason the Mongols always moved with a great number of horses to use as remounts. During a campaign all hands were mobilized, and if necessary even women and children took part in the combat. The great mobility of the Mongols was enhanced also by their use of yurts, the characteristic felt tents of the Inner Asian nomads, which were quickly pulled down and just as easily reassembled.

Their method of attack is well known. They fatigued the enemy by forcing him into several fruitless attacks against their highly mobile and elusive cavalry. The Mongols then made a mock retreat pursued by their adversary, who would usually break ranks. Suddenly they returned to the attack, scattering the surprised and by now exhausted enemy, and showering him with arrows. The final assault was accompanied by deafening shouts and the terrifying noise of the 'whistling arrows' used by the nomads since early times but unknown in the West. The piercing sound was produced by holes made in the arrow head.

The Mongols improved their system of warfare by adopt-

ing techniques from other countries, such as the use of mangonels which they learned from the Chinese, and battering
rams and incendiaries made with naphtha (sometimes human fat) and thrown with catapults, which they probably
took from the Persians. They also used dummies made of felt
and propped on their horses to deceive the enemy as to their
real strength.

Often, when attacking, they would place their prisoners of
war in the front line, a cruel but effective device to confuse
the enemy and hamper his actions. Contrary to the usual
practice in Europe at the time, the Mongol military leaders
did not personally take part in the fight, but directed the
operations from a safe distance. These various techniques
undoubtedly made Chingis Khan's army the most efficient
war machine in the world before the modern age, and one
that always fills us with wonder, considering that its creator
was, unlike Alexander and Caesar, an illiterate barbarian to
the end of his days.

The conquest of Central and Western Asia was not followed by a regular occupation of the country by the Mongols. When Chingis Khan returned to his native Mongolia in
1225, he took his army with him, leaving behind only a few
military governors as representatives of his power and as tax-
collectors. The invading horde had barely left Persia when
Jalal al-Din returned from Delhi in a bid to reunify the
country under his rule. His task was made easier by the fame
he had acquired in his early exploits against the Mongols,
and by the latter's temporary loss of interest in the affairs of
Central Asia.

Chingis Khan's mind was now set again on China, where
his generals had made little progress during his ten years'
absence. The Hsi-Hsia kingdom was the major obstacle. Its
king had not fulfilled his promise to help Chingis with troops

during the Khorezmian war and had now become definitely hostile. He had to be dealt with before any progress could be made against the Jurchen.

The war against Hsi-Hsia was the last campaign of the Mongol warrior. He died in August 1227 during the military operations in northwest China and only a few months before his generals conquered the Hsi-Hsia kingdom. He was only sixty.

THE CRISIS IN EUROPE: CHURCH VERSUS EMPIRE

The thorny issue of the succession to the throne and the resumption of the war against the Chin kingdom diverted the Mongols' attention from the West for several years. In the meantime Europe was left wondering about the identity of the mysterious people who had so suddenly appeared at the fringes of civilization leaving havoc and death in their wake, and disappearing again, just as suddenly, into the unknown.

The Russians, who were among the main sufferers of the unexpected incursion, were as puzzled as everybody else. The anonymous author of the *Novgorodian Chronicle* laconically says: 'And the Tatars turned back from the river Dnieper, and we know not whence they came, nor where they hid themselves again; God knows whence he fetched them against us.' The current reports about Prester John and King David only added to the confusion. Küchlüg, the original King David, was dead by now, but an even fiercer enemy of Islam had appeared in the heart of Asia in the person of Chingis Khan. News of the war in Khorezm had reached Syria and Byzantium, and thence Europe, where everyone assumed that King David had launched it and was personally directing it.

Pope Honorius III, who early in 1221 had learned through

58

Cardinal Pelagius and James of Vitry about the *Report on King David*, saw in this news a confirmation of its contents. He was so convinced of its truth that in the following months he repeatedly announced to Europe the victorious progress of King David in Persia and the forthcoming liberation of the Holy Land. The failure to appear when he was most needed did not shake Europe's faith in the existence of King David, and when, two years later, the Mongols invaded south Russia their raid was also ascribed to him.

In 1223 the king of Hungary, Andreas II (1202–35), informed the pope about the coming into Russia of 'a certain King David or, as he is more usually called, Prester John', with a multitude of people. The report went on to say that King David had left India seven years earlier, taking with him the body of the Apostle Thomas, and in a single day his troops had killed 200,000 Russians and Comans.

Characteristically, this semi-fictional account found more credence than a realistic description of the Mongols given by Rusudan (1223–45), the famous queen of Georgia, in a letter sent to the pope in the same year.

What could the West make out of these curious and conflicting reports? One thing became slowly and painfully clear: King David, whether himself identical with or a descendant of Prester John, could not be as Christian as the current accounts claimed, in spite of his obvious hatred for the Moslems. The ruthlessness displayed by his soldiers in Georgia and in the Caucasus was considered excessive even by the contemporary European conception of warfare. Doubts about the Christianity of the Mongols were expressed by the French monk Alberic of Trois Fontaines (*d.* 1241), author of one of the most important chronicles of this period. Unfortunately for the chroniclers, but not Europe, the Mongols left without trace, and no confirmation or disproof of

59

Asia in the Thirt

Fourteenth Centuries

these reports was therefore possible. Because of this, as Alberic says, the rumours 'vanished in no time'.

The rumours did, indeed, subside for a while, but the recent events had nevertheless shaken Europe's confidence, particularly as they followed the dismal failure of the Fifth Crusade on which were pinned so many hopes. The most obvious result of the crisis was the worsening of relations between the papacy and the Holy Roman Empire.

As is known, the conflict which opposed the successors of St. Peter to those of Charlemagne goes back to the Investiture Controversy of the eleventh century and the formulation, by Pope Gregory VII (1073–85), of the doctrine that the Church exerts universal rule over the whole of Christendom, including kings and emperors. The Hohenstaufen emperor Frederick I had, like Henry IV, rejected this theocratic idea and had actually taken arms against the pope, but it was his grandson Frederick II (1194–1250) who widened the breach until it became irreparable. His reluctance to join the Crusade in 1218 after having taken the vow three years earlier was undoubtedly one of the causes of its failure. However, the good Pope Honorius, who had been a tutor of Frederick and was genuinely fond of him, had always been willing to accept his excuses, and this attitude had encouraged the young and eccentric monarch to pursue his independent policy.

Bred in the semi-oriental atmosphere of the Norman court at Palermo, Frederick combined brilliant intellectual powers with a deep love for Arabic culture and an insatiable curiosity for the strange and exotic. He had a sensual, cruel, egotistic and extremely complex nature. His sympathies for Islam together with the Hohenstaufen traditional antagonism to the Church had made him from the beginning the *enfant terrible* of Europe.

Honorius died in 1227. His successor Gregory IX (*d.* 1241), a stern and uncompromising pope, had little tolerance for the emperor's whims and erratic behaviour. After a further delay in sailing for the Holy Land in 1227, Gregory excommunicated him, thus automatically banning him from the Crusade. Frederick, nevertheless, sailed forth the following year at the head of a small force. So took place that paradoxical Sixth Crusade during which, in the space of a few months, the excommunicated emperor secured for the Christians the possession of Jerusalem, Nazareth, Bethlehem, as well as the territory between Jerusalem and Acre. This astonishing feat, achieved without the shedding of blood, was the result of Frederick's subtle diplomatic work with the Sultan of Egypt, al-Kamil. The negotiations were also made easier by the sultan's genuine fear of imminent danger from the east. The cause of such fear was none other than Jalal al-Din of Khorezm who by 1225 had become master of western Persia and Azerbaijan. He had then attacked Baghdad and Georgia, posing in this way a direct threat to the Armenian possessions of al-Kamil's brother al-Ashraf. This threat, and dissension within the family of al-Kamil (his other brother, al-Mu'azzam of Syria, was a supporter of Jalal al-Din), favoured Frederick's political game and account for the sultan's willingness to secure peace, even at great cost, with the European powers. It is worth noting that the success of the Sixth Crusade was ultimately due to the westward push of the Khorezmian prince which, in turn, had been caused by the Mongol invasion.

Although Frederick's bloodless Crusade was followed by a reconciliation with the pope, with absolution and formal peace (Treaty of San Germano, July 1230), the relations between Church and Empire were hopelessly damaged. It was only a matter of time before the uneasy truce would once again turn into open conflict. Frederick's active anti-clericalism at home and his uncompromising attitude towards the Frankish barons of *Outremer*, whose assizes he opposed with the feudal law of Sicily, soon wiped out most of the prestige and political gains that the Crusade had earned him.

THE ELECTION OF ÖGÖDEI AND THE CONQUEST OF CHIN

While Europe was busy debating Frederick's actions, the Mongols were engaged in their own controversy over the election of the khan to succeed Chingis. The issue was a difficult one for, according to Mongol law, the new emperor had to be elected by the great assembly of princes and nobles (*quriltai*). However, according to an ancient custom, the youngest son was favoured in so far as he inherited as 'guardian of the hearth' the home grounds and possessions, i.e. the most important share of the family patrimony. Now Chingis Khan had apparently contradicted both principles by naming his third son Ögödei (1229–41) as his successor.

When, in 1228, the Mongol military leaders and grandees gathered at Köde'e Aral, a plain in the Tsenker–Kerulen region, a split took place within the assembly, a section of which opposed the candidature of Ögödei with that of Tolui, the fourth and youngest son of Chingis Khan. The conservative faction was overruled by the upholders of Chingis's will, and Ögödei was eventually enthroned in September 1229. The election caused a rift between the two branches of the imperial family which led, thirty years later, to the replacement of Ögödei's line by that of Tolui.

At the death of Chingis his vast empire was divided into dominions (*ulus*) among his four sons. By an extension of the law of ultimogeniture Jochi, as the eldest son, received the

64

furthermost domain which embraced all the territories between the river Irtysh, the Aral and the Volga. As we have
already seen, Jochi was the one who in 1223 had led the raid
upon Russia, and it is quite possible that the real motivation
of the raid was the acquisition of an *ulus* for his house. However, as he had died shortly before Chingis, the dominion
passed to his son Batu (1227–54). Chaghatai, the second son,
received Transoxiana and the former Qara-Khitai and
Uighur territories. Ögödei received the former Naiman country in western Mongolia and Kazakhstan (north and east of
Lake Balkash), and Tolui the Mongolian homeland. In this
way the imperial princes all became khans of their respective
domains. This is why the title held by the Mongol emperors
after Chingis was the Turkish title *khaghan* 'khan of khans',
or Great Khan, as Marco Polo renders it.

The court was empowered to distribute the revenue collected by Mongol governors from the subject populations
amongst the imperial relatives and the Mongol nobility.
Thus Chingis Khan's conquests had the effect of transforming
a nomadic and semi-nomadic tribal society into a kind of
feudal society in which the military leaders (*noyad*) enjoyed
the fruits of their conquests without having to relinquish
their traditional mode of life. This new steppe nobility, whose
most prominent representatives were, of course, Chingis's
clansmen and early companions, and the élite members of
the Imperial Guard, also exacted goods and service from the
Mongol tribesmen according to the privileges conferred on
them by Chingis in 1206. However, the continuous military
campaigns waged by the Mongols placed a heavy burden on
the common tribesman, as they forced him to spend more
and more of his time fighting or preparing for war, and less
and less in cattle-breeding and domestic occupations. This
phenomenon, coupled with the considerable loss in lives

incurred by the Mongols, compelled their leaders to rely increasingly on slave labour at home and on foreign troops in their campaigns abroad. Massive deportations of civilians, especially craftsmen, were carried out in Chingis Khan's time. These unfortunate people, forcibly removed from their towns and villages in Persia and north China, were resettled in Siberia and Mongolia where they had to weave, mine and make tools and weapons for their oppressive masters. Some of these settlements grew and became towns, but on the whole the system of mass deportations did not prove very satisfactory. To remove large groups of people to distant areas was not practical as the uprooting impaired their productivity. The Mongols realized this and gradually changed their policy, concentrating more on the exploitation of the settled population of the conquered territories. Lacking the necessary administrative skill themselves to carry out this task, they had to make use of literate captives and defectors. They also exempted the clergy of the conquered countries from taxes and compulsory service, and in this way obtained the co-operation of the local Churches in keeping the people in subjection. Thus began that policy of religious toleration which in time became one of the main features of Mongol rule.

When Ögödei was elected in 1229, one of his first tasks was to work out a more efficient system of levying taxes and corvée from his subjects in order to carry out the programme of military conquest launched by his father. Ögödei was, for a Mongol, a benign monarch, generous and ready to accept advice from the expert. At his court—the imperial camp was at Karakorum, some 200 miles southwest of present Ulanbator—there were Chinese scholars serving as scribes and astrologers, Christian Kereit and Uighur advisers versed in the languages and cultures of Central Asia, as well as a large group of Central and Western Asian Moslems engaged in trade operations for the Mongols. With the help of these people, Ögödei set up in 1231 a State Secretariat to deal with the administration of his vast empire. A more regular system of taxation was introduced for the Mongols and their subjects in China and Central Asia, and a complex network of post-relay stations was established to ensure quick and efficient communications throughout the realm. This was one of Ögödei's greatest achievements, and one of which he himself was justly proud.

At the same time the new emperor reorganized the army in order to incorporate foreign elements. Troops were levied in occupied territories and the native officers who had defected to the Mongols were put in charge of them. The war against Chin and the subsequent conquest of China were carried out mainly with these auxiliary troops made up of northern Chinese, Hsi-Hsia and Khitan effectives. There were still thousands of Khitans living in north China, and from the beginning of the Mongol invasion they had sided with the Mongols against their Jurchen overlords. The Mongols appreciated their action and rewarded the Khitan noblemen with high positions in the army and at court. One of the chief advisers of Chingis Khan and Ögödei was a sinicized Khitan by the name of Yeh-lü Ch'u-ts'ai (1189–1243). He played a major role in reducing the devastation of China by showing that the Mongols would gain more through a rational exploitation of the country than by the reckless destruction of its human and natural resources.

In 1230 the enlarged Mongol army led by Ögödei and his top generals, chief among whom was Sübötei, resumed its offensive against Chin. The territory to be conquered south of Peking and beyond the Yellow River was vast and well defended. The Jurchen, who realized that this time the Mongols were determined to annihilate them, fought desperately.

In besieging the Chin strongholds, like the new capital Kai-feng in Honan, the Mongol forces employed mangonels throwing large stones; they also dug mine-tunnels and built special siege-towers. Kaifeng was captured by Sübötei in 1233, and its population, about four million people, was saved only thanks to the personal intercession of Yeh-lü Ch'u-ts'ai. Still the Jurchen, undaunted, continued to fight. They had not reckoned, however, with the Sung court which saw in the Jurchen's predicament the perfect opportunity to dispose of them. Caught between the Mongol army in the north and the Sung troops in the south, the Chin forces were over-whelmed. In 1234 the Chin emperor committed suicide in his last stronghold and both his dynasty and his kingdom came to an end.

The occupation of the Hsi-Hsia and Chin kingdoms, i.e. of the northern half of China, brought the Mongols in direct contact with the Sung empire which occupied the southern half of the country. A confrontation between the two powers was inevitable. After a few fruitless embassies sent to claim a larger share of the former Jurchen territory, the Sung took the initiative and rashly attacked the Mongols in Honan. The Mongols were no doubt waiting for this, and at the great assembly at Karakorum in 1235 Ögödei solemnly declared war on Sung.

THE MONGOL INVASION OF RUSSIA: FIRST REACTIONS IN WESTERN EUROPE

At the same assembly Ögödei also decided to send a large army to conquer Europe. This decision, which was to have such dramatic consequences for the Western world, deserves closer scrutiny. Shortly after his enthronement and on the eve of his invasion of China, Ögödei had sent a small army, led by General Chormaghan, to put an end to Jalal al-Din's activity in Persia. So great was the terror inspired by the Mongols that at the news of their arrival Jalal al-Din's followers hastily abandoned him. The last sultan of Khorezm fled to the mountains of Kurdistan where he met his death at the hand of a local peasant in August 1231.

Chormaghan then began to restore Mongol control in northwestern Persia and in the neighbouring countries of Georgia and Greater Armenia. The limited capability of his army (about 30,000 men) prevented him, however, from extending his operations farther into the Caucasus and in Mesopotamia. But the Mongol *Drang nach Westen* policy was now part of a grandiose plan of world conquest bequeathed by Chingis. At the Mongol court in Karakorum a strong militant faction urged the implementation of the late emperor's will. Ögödei, however, was not very enthusiastic about sending a large expeditionary force to the west. Not only did the war against Sung promise to be long and troublesome, but the Mongols were already experiencing at the time great difficulties in conquering Korea, which they had invaded in 1231. Ögödei was also beginning to show the effects of his addiction to liquor by gradually withdrawing from active leadership and letting secretaries, protégés and female relatives take over the administration. In the end, under pressure from his younger brother Möngke, who was a great upholder of Chingis's principles, and Batu, who saw in the western campaign an excellent opportunity to extend his possessions, Ögödei gave his approval to the invasion and entrusted Batu with the command of the operations. An army of 150,000 men was to be raised with levies from all four dominions and placed under the orders of General Sübötei. Ögödei's sons Güyüg and Qadan, as well as several other members of the imperial family, joined the expedition.

Ögödei himself remained at Karakorum, which in 1235 had been consecrated capital of the empire with the construction of a royal palace and the erection of a wall around the city. Except for a few buildings, mainly halls and temples, erected by Chinese and Persian architects, Karakorum retained its character of a tent settlement and was probably not very dissimilar from nineteenth-century Urga.

After several months' preparation the Mongol army, which included Turkish and other auxiliary troops, began its operations in the territory between the Aral and the upper course of the Volga, home of the Kangli Turks, the Bashkirs and the so-called Volga Bulgars. The area of southwestern Siberia where the still semi-nomadic and shamanistic Bashkirs lived, i.e. the region of present-day Orenburg, was the Magna Hungaria, or Greater Hungary, of our medieval authors. It owed its name to the belief, not yet disproved, that it was the original home of the Magyar tribes that had occupied Hungary at the end of the ninth century. The Volga Bulgars, who lived mostly along the Kama river and in the area of modern Kazan, were likewise the descendants of Turkish tribes related to those that had invaded eastern Europe and settled in Bulgaria in the seventh century. These Bulgars of Greater Bulgaria, as their country was then called, had been engaged for several centuries in trade between Central Asia and northern Europe, and their capital Bulgar, at the confluence of the two rivers, was a prosperous commercial centre.

The Bashkirs and the Volga Bulgars were the first target of the Mongol army and bore the brunt of the onslaught. Bulgar was sacked and the whole territory was horribly devastated. The Mongols had not forgotten that on their return journey after the raid in Russia in 1223 the Bulgars had attacked the troops of Sübötei causing considerable loss of lives. This time they made sure that there would be no repetition of the incident.

Having crushed all local resistance in the Volga region, the Mongols in 1237–38 attacked the Comans of the lower Don, many of whom surrendered and joined their army. A large group of them escaped to Hungary and placed themselves under the protection of King Béla IV (1235–70).

While the rearguard was thus being secured, another army pushed northwards towards Riazan on the Oka river. The old city was captured and sacked in December 1237. Then it was the turn of Moscow, Suzdal and Vladimir, which were burned and destroyed in February of the following year. The leader of the Russian princes, Grand Duke Iuri II, perished shortly after in a battle on the Sit' river (4 March 1238).

The last metropolis to fall to the Mongols was Kiev, 'the mother of Russian cities' and residence of the head of the Greek Orthodox Church in Russia, which was taken and destroyed after a short but desperate resistance on 6 December 1240. This brought to an end the Kievan Period of Russian history (878–1240): from now on the centre of political gravity in Russia was to move northeast.

Most of the west Russian princes escaped to Hungary and Poland, and before long their relentless pursuers advanced into Galicia, while almost simultaneously another army crossed the frozen Vistula and penetrated into Poland.

The threat to western Europe was now great and immediate. Russia's remoteness, political fragmentation and, chiefly, her adherence to a schismatic Church, had kept her estranged from the rest of Europe. Her present plight was viewed by some of her neighbours, the Swedes and the Teutonic Knights in particular, with considerable satisfaction. However, an attack on Poland and Hungary, both Catholic countries in close relations with Rome, was a different matter. King Béla, whose long reign was a dramatic exercise in survival, had had an early presentiment that the Mongols would return and that Hungary, because of her geographical position, would be one of the main victims of the barbarian horsemen. The invasion of Attila's Huns in the fourth and fifth centuries, and that of the Magyars themselves in the ninth century, were two notable precedents, as Béla knew only too well.

Moreover, Hungary had been for some time in close relation with the Comans. Dominican friars had been sent by King Andreas II to evangelize their tribes as early as 1221; subsequently, several converted Coman chieftains had declared themselves loyal to the Hungarian monarch. Béla, who had assumed also the title of King of the Comans, had actually tried to establish a closer link with both the Comans and the Bashkirs of Greater Hungary in order to create a unified political and religious barrier against future Mongol attacks. Several missions led by mendicant friars, mainly Dominicans, were sent by Béla to explore the situation during the 'thirties. The most famous of these missions is that of Friar Julian, to which we have already referred. Although in 1237 Julian was forced to turn back by the oncoming Mongols, he was able to question two envoys sent by Batu to Béla who had been intercepted on their way to Hungary by Grand Duke Iuri. He then hastily returned to Hungary to report to the king and break the news of the impending calamity to the rest of Europe.

As mentioned earlier, Friar Julian's report deals also with the expansionist programme of the Mongols. Julian actually claims that their aim is world domination, with Rome as the goal of the next invasion. This is the first clear reference in the West to the Mongols' true ambition of becoming the masters of Europe as well as of Asia. It is worth noting that

Julian, who writes in Latin, calls the Mongols 'Tartari', i.e. Tartars. Here we also have one of the first instances of the use of this term, which from now on will be the regular name of the Mongols in Europe. At the time of the invasion the general designation of Tatars for the Mongols penetrated into Europe, almost certainly through the Comans. However, it was immediately changed into 'Tartars' because of the latter's association with the Latin word *tartarus* meaning 'hell' (Hades). In popular imagination the fierce Mongols were in fact pictured as devils released from hell. The term Tartar became current in Italian, French and English, while the form Tatar was retained in German and in the eastern European languages.

In spite of the literary elements still embedded in it, the image of the Mongols in the West was gradually becoming true to reality. Very real indeed was the letter which the two Mongol ambassadors captured by Iuri were to deliver to the Hungarian king. Its content is also recorded by Friar Julian. The message refers to the asylum granted by Béla to the Coman refugees, and to the detention of some Mongol envoys who had apparently been sent earlier to Hungary. The words of warning contained in Batu's letter were intended as an ultimatum, but probably because of the rhetorical style peculiar to all Mongol official documents Béla failed to realize that what the Mongols demanded was nothing short of unconditional surrender. If the latter's claim that the king had harmed several of their envoys was true, then Hungary's fate was already sealed.

On Julian's return, Béla transmitted the information brought by the friar to his uncle Berthold of Andechs, Patriarch of Aquileia, and to Salvio Salvi, Bishop of Perugia and papal legate to Hungary. He also informed the Bishop of Brixen and the Count of Tirol, warning them of a possible invasion from the east and the north. Julian himself reported to the Curia in Rome. Thus by the end of 1237, both the pope and Frederick were all aware of the Tartar threat. According to Alberic of Trois Fontaines, the emperor had also received in this year an order of submission from the Mongols. This was accompanied by an offer to assume office under them. Frederick is reported to have replied, in his characteristic fashion, that being an expert bird hunter he could have easily become the khan's falconer! One is left with the impression that the idea of a barbarian invasion, which would no doubt have caused embarrassment to the Church and Christian Europe, was not too displeasing to the emperor who, therefore, had little desire to do anything to prevent it.

The pope, for his part, had resumed his controversy with Frederick over the launching of a new Crusade (the treaty with al-Kamil expired in 1239) and was so engrossed in his effort to undermine the emperor's authority that he paid too little attention to Béla's warning letters, and to the many requests for help that reached the West from peoples immediately threatened by the Mongol invasion.

The dissident Oriental Christians, such as the Jacobites and Nestorians, had sent representatives with proposals for a reunion with the Church of Rome. Queen Rusudan of Georgia had protested her Christian allegiance in a desperate plea for assistance from the pope. Apparently even the leader of the Ismaili Assassins, the dreaded 'Old Man of the Mountain', had sent emissaries in 1238 asking the European nations to join him in a grand alliance against the common foe. The comment of Peter des Roches, Bishop of Winchester, to this request is well known: 'let us leave these dogs to devour one another, that they may all be consumed, and perish; and we, when we proceed against the enemies of Christ who remain, will slay them, and cleanse the face of the earth, so that all

74

the world will be subject to the one Catholic Church, and there will be one shepherd and one fold.'

One cannot help feeling, reading the many contemporary accounts, that the papacy viewed these protestations of faith and requests for help as a sign that a return to the fold of the Eastern Churches was imminent, and that the Mongol invasion, which was the prime cause of all these sudden changes, was a providential act. We must not forget that so far the Tartar scourge had hit only the Moslems and the Christian schismatic communities of the Near East and Russia. Moreover, the whole question of Prester John and King David was far from being settled and doubts still lingered in the minds of many people about the faith of the invaders. Thus, instead of preaching a crusade against the Mongols, Pope Gregory went ahead with his preparations for the next Crusade against Egypt, after having duly excommunicated Frederick, for the second time, in March 1239.

III

Ad Tartaros!

THE MONGOLS IN POLAND AND HUNGARY

While Tibald of Champagne's knights were engaged in that costly and futile expedition in Egypt and Palestine known as the French Crusade (1239–40), some fifteen hundred miles farther north the Mongols were plundering the Russian principalities and preparing for their invasion of central and southern Europe.

The Mongol advance corps that had penetrated into Poland at the beginning of 1241 sacked Sandomir and Cracow, and on 9 April they defeated the joint forces of the Poles and the Teutonic Knights at Wahlstadt near Legnica (Liegnitz). The Polish chroniclers relate how on this occasion the Mongols used, for the first time, a smoke-producing device, probably of Chinese origin, which caused disarray among the Western forces. This ingenious contraption was in the shape of a large black standard surmounted by a bearded head whose mouth exhaled poisonous gases. Nevertheless, the Mongols also suffered grave losses. After the fierce battle the Mongol soldiers cut one ear off every enemy corpse and filled nine large bags with them. From Silesia they turned south into Moravia to join the armies led by Batu and Sübötei for an all-out attack on Buda. Meanwhile, in an equally fierce battle at Mohi on the river Sajó Batu's forces defeated the hundred-thousand strong Magyar army led by King Béla (11 April). The Hungarians were cut to pieces and the unfortunate king had to flee for his life to the relative safety of Croatia, from where he sent urgent pleas for help to the emperor, the pope and the kings of Europe.

The Mongol horsemen now proceeded to pillage methodically Bohemia and Moravia, showing every sign of settling for good in the inviting Hungarian *puszta*, so reminiscent of their native steppeland. They even began striking coins. On Christmas Day 1241 Batu's forces crossed the frozen Danube, seized Buda and burned it.

The widespread destruction, the massacres of entire populations and the indiscriminate rape and plunder that accompanied the Mongol invasion are known to us from contemporary Polish chronicles, the chronicles of Alberic of Trois Fontaines and Matthew Paris, and a number of eye-witnesses' reports, such as the three letters of Friar Jordan of Giano (*c.* 1195–1262), Provincial Vicar of the Franciscan Order in Bohemia and Poland, and Canon Roger's *Plaintive Song on the Destruction of the Kingdom of Hungary by the Tartars*.

These last documents occupy a special place for their graphic description of the Tartars' progress. They illustrate, once more, the prominent part played by ecclesiastics in collecting and transmitting information about the Mongols. Monks and clerics were, of course, in an ideal position to do this, as their churches and convents became in time of danger shelters for refugees from different parts of the country; moreover, the vast ecclesiastical network to which they belonged commanded what was probably the most efficient system of communication in the West. The medieval monastery thus combined also the functions of news agency and recording office, and the major chronicles of this period, including those mentioned above, are in fact the product of patient monastic labour.

Friar Jordan's letters, dating from the first half of 1241 and addressed to all the Christians, to Henry II, Duke of Brabant, and to his Order, vividly describe the Mongols' ravages in Poland and Hungary and the nature of the enemy: 'they cross with incredible speed [so Jordan writes] the swiftest rivers and the thickest forests. . . . They put people to the sword regardless of age, condition or sex and profane the places consecrated to God . . . where they camp with their women, tying their horses to the tombs of the saints, whose bodies they expose to animals and birds. . . . The mere sound of their name sets the crowds to flight. . . . Their women, armed, ride horses and spare no one; she who fights best is regarded as the most desirable, just as in our country she who weaves and sews best is more desired than the prettier one.'

In his letters Jordan also describes the Mongols' characteristic way of feigning retreat when confronted with superior forces and then suddenly returning and charging, their use of war machines, their system of placing prisoners in the front line and of incorporating in their armies the people who have submitted to them, like the Comans.

In 1242, or shortly after, the *Plaintive Song* (*Miserabile Carmen*) began circulating in Europe. This is the dramatic personal narrative of Roger of Apulia, Canon of Varazdin and later Archbishop of Spalato (*d.* 1266). Roger had been captured by the Mongols in Hungary. After several months spent in abject servitude and terror he eventually succeeded in escaping, almost miraculously, from his captors. In his *Song* he relates in great detail the progress of the invading horde, the cunning stratagems devised by the Mongols to obtain the capitulation of the towns they besieged, the com-

78

position of their army and their inexorable treatment of prisoners, something of which he had first-hand experience. His account completes the picture painted by Friar Jordan of Giano. From him we learn, for instance, how renegades from various European countries, including one from England, also fought on the side of the Mongols.

By this time, and chiefly through Hungarian sources, news of the Tartar onslaught had spread far and wide in Europe. The response to Béla's frantic appeals ranged from sympathy over his misfortune to outright blame for his carelessness, but no one came forward with a practical suggestion or a definite offer of assistance. The pope and Frederick used the invasion of Hungary as just another pretext for mutual recriminations in a series of claims and counterclaims addressed to the European monarchs whose support they were eager to win. In a widely circulated *Letter Against the Tartars* which, incidentally, betrays a remarkable knowledge about them, the emperor accused the pontiff of wrecking the unity of the Christian princes by his attacks on him, thus preventing Europe from joining forces against the common foe. To show his willingness to help Hungary and Poland, Frederick ordered his son Conrad to mobilize the German army. A great sum was levied for this purpose, but the army never took the field. This, however, did not prevent Conrad from claiming later to have inflicted a severe defeat on the Mongols and to have been responsible for their withdrawal from Europe!

Pope Gregory countered the charges by accusing the emperor of having a secret understanding with the Mongols, for whose coming Frederick alone was to be held responsible. To Béla the pope offered words of consolation similar to those forwarded earlier to Queen Rusudan, promising to help the king immediately after his victory over Frederick.

Gregory was genuinely grieved, but his bitter dispute with the emperor overshadowed all other considerations and prevented him from taking more positive steps.

The reaction of Louis IX of France, the future St. Louis, was pious but also of little practical value. To his mother, Queen Blanche, he replied: 'May comfort from Heaven raise us up, my mother, and if these people, whom we call Tartars, should come upon us, either we will thrust them back into the regions of Tartarus, whence they emanated, or else they shall send all of us to Heaven.'

Others, like Duke Frederick of Austria, took advantage of Béla's plight to occupy some of the eastern districts of Hungary. As for England, Henry III felt he had no need to respond, as his country was not directly affected by the Tartar peril. Only in 1238 had the Mongol invasion briefly made itself felt in England, when the attack on the Russian cities threatened Novgorod's commercial enterprises in the Baltic and North Seas. As a result, the German fish merchants had not gone, as usual, to Yarmouth to buy herrings and that year England had a glut of fish which made history. Edward Gibbon, writing in the eighteenth century, was still amused by the fact that an order of the Mongol emperor living in the Far East should have lowered the price of herrings on the English market!

Disunity in the Western camp not only compromised the chances of rallying to the help of the Hungarian monarch, but it also made the whole of Europe dangerously open to the Mongol onslaught. The Mongol detachment sent in pursuit of Béla was soon in Croatia. Zagreb was captured, but the king fled to Dalmatia, always followed by the enemy. At Spalato (Split) Béla took a ship and, like Sultan Muhammad of Khorezm twenty years before, escaped to an offshore island. The Mongols could no longer reach him.

The angry pursuers then devastated the coast as far south as Montenegro. In the meantime a Mongol expeditionary force was sent from Hungary to Austria in preparation for a full-scale attack.

WESTERN EUROPE'S NARROW ESCAPE

At no other time in history was the Christian world so close to disaster. In the spring of 1242 the Mongols were at Klosterneuburg, only a few miles from Vienna, when suddenly, and for no apparent reason, the attack was called off and all their armies in central Europe were withdrawn.

This sudden retreat was regarded by the puzzled and frightened Europe as something very close to a miracle. It was actually due to the death of the Great Khan Ögödei (11 December 1241), news of which had just reached the armies in the field. The presence of all the princes and military leaders was immediately required for the convocation of the *quriltai* that had to elect the new emperor.

Ögödei had been killed by excessive drinking. He was especially fond of grape-wine which was brought to him from Central Asia, and which he apparently preferred to kumys (fermented mare's milk), the traditional beverage of the Inner Asian nomads. The latter part of Ögödei's reign had been marked by a worsening in the relations between the sons and grandsons of Chingis Khan and by a progressive deterioration of Mongol administrative practices. After a successful attempt by statesmen like Yeh-lü Ch'u-ts'ai in China and Mahmud Yalawach in Persia to rationalize the exploitation of the conquered territories, the Mongol court's increasing need of goods and wealth had prompted Ögödei to follow the advice of some Moslem merchants at court to increase the quota of tax and tributes levied on the people.

Effective authority at Karakorum in this period was in the hands of Ögödei's wife Töregene, a fierce and rapacious woman. After the emperor's death and during the period of her regency (1241–46) she dismissed all his former chancellors and replaced them with her protégés. Ögödei had nominated his grandson Shiremün as successor, but Töregene wanted her own son Güyüg, who was Ögödei's eldest son, on the throne, and she spared no efforts to foster his candidature. The court was split into factions and riddled with intrigues. Batu disliked both her and Güyüg, with whom he had quarrelled during the Russian campaign, and was determined to oppose his election. He gave, therefore, his weighty support to the rival branch of Tolui which had been defeated at the *quriltai* of 1229. As Tolui had died a few years before, also of alcoholism, he backed the candidature of his son Möngke. The Chaghataid branch of the family sided against him and supported the Ögödeids. The ensuing quarrel delayed the convocation of the diet, and it was not until 1246 that the great *quriltai* finally assembled near Karakorum to elect the new khaghan.

In the meantime the shrewd Batu had consolidated his position as the Mongol 'ruler of the West' by incorporating the recently conquered territories of south Russia in his dominion. This became the Khanate of Kipchak, later known as the Golden Horde. His early headquarters were at Bulgar on the upper Volga. Subsequently Batu moved his tents farther down the river, first in the area of Saratov, then near the present village of Selitrennoye on the Akhtuba. This became the town of Sarai (Persian for 'Palace'), later called Old Sarai or Sarai-Batu to distinguish it from Sarai-Berke or New Sarai founded by Batu's brother Berke (1257–66). New Sarai was on the site of the modern town of Tsarev near Volgograd. Old Sarai, however, remained the capital of the Golden Horde until the reign of Özbeg (1313–41). It was here that the Russian princes had to pay homage to the Mongol overlords and have their investiture confirmed.

In Russia the 'Tartar yoke' lasted two and a half centuries. During the first hundred years of Mongol domination, the Russian subjects had to pay a heavy tribute to the Golden Horde. This harsh economic exploitation, added to the earlier destruction of flourishing centres such as Kiev, and the subsequent isolation from the rest of Europe, had the effect of plunging Russia into a culturally dark age. Hence it is small wonder that most of her historians regard the period of Tartar rule as an unparalleled calamity, even though it led to the formation of the Muscovite state and the eventual political unification of the country.

Although most of Europe was fortunately spared the fate of Russia, the Mongols' presence beyond the river Dnieper and the fact that their power was felt as far north as Lithuania and as far south as Bulgaria could not fail to create an acute awareness of peril, which the reports from Hungary did nothing to dispel. It was widely believed that the Mongol withdrawal was only temporary and that they would soon return to complete their destructive task. This feeling of impending doom was largely generated by the sad state of disorder in the Church and the growing conviction that the Tartars, as instruments of Divine Providence, had descended on Europe to administer a salutary punishment on all Christendom. Hence the name 'hammer of God' often applied to them at the time. For some the Mongols were none other than the biblical people of Gog and Magog released from their segregation in the Caucasus, their invasion heralding the coming of the Antichrist and the end of the world. Amidst such conflicting and uncertain theories the leaders of the time were clearly unable to cope with the situation.

INNOCENT IV's EMBASSIES TO THE TARTARS

Pope Gregory IX died in August 1241. His successor Celestin IV occupied the Chair of Peter for only seventeen days. Owing to Frederick's interference it was not until June 1243 that a new pontiff was elected. The choice fell on Sinibaldo Fieschi, an eminent Genoese jurist, who took the name of Innocent IV (1243–54). On his accession Innocent found Europe spiritually divided and under the threat of renewed devastations. The Holy Land, after the fruitless French expedition, was torn by internal quarrels, and his own domains in Italy had been invaded by the emperor.

In July 1244 the situation came to a head. Jerusalem was attacked by Khorezmian troops, formerly in the service of Jalal al-Din, called in by Sultan Ayyub of Syria. The city was captured by the Turks and thoroughly sacked. This disaster was followed a few months later by the destruction of the Frankish army at Gaza which practically sealed the fate of Jerusalem. The Holy City was never to be recovered by the Christians.

In Italy, a short-lived agreement between Innocent and Frederick signed in March 1244 broke down in the summer of the same year. With the collapse of the negotiations with the emperor, Innocent's attempt to preach a new Crusade was thwarted by fresh hostilities and rebellion in Rome. Fearing for his own safety, the pope left Italy and repaired to Lyons. There, under the protection of King Louis, he immediately convoked a General Council for June 1245.

The main items on the agenda for this, the XIII Ecumenical Council, were the deposition of the emperor, the launching of the Crusade and 'seeking a remedy against the Tartars'. To safeguard Europe from a new Tartar invasion was in fact one of Innocent's chief concerns. He was well aware that the future security of Christendom depended largely on the satisfactory solution of this problem. While fostering unity among all the countries endangered by the Mongols and strengthening their defences, it was also imperative to find out without delay who these Mongols really were and what were their intentions. It was with this aim in mind that Innocent sent a number of exploratory missions to the East a few months before the Council was to meet. These he entrusted to Dominican and Franciscan friars.

Like the contemporary Order of Friars Minor founded by St. Francis, the Dominican Order, or Order of Friars Preachers, was young and vigorous and its members filled with religious enthusiasm. Its founder, St. Dominic (1170–1221), had set as the principal function of the Order the defence of the faith and the conversion of the heathen. Both these aims were pursued by the Preachers with alacrity and, at times, over-zealous fervour as displayed, for instance, in the ruthless suppression of the Albigenses.

Dominican missionaries were the first to evangelize the pagan people of eastern Europe and Kipchak—a task especially assigned to the Hungarian friars of the Order—and together with the Franciscans we find them actively engaged in the Middle East already during the time of Gregory IX. Here, in the Province of Terra Santa, Preachers and Minorites pursued a two-fold policy: to convert the Moslems and pagans, and bring about the reunion of the Eastern Christians, such as the Nestorians, the Jacobites and so on, to the Catholic Church. This unprecedented missionary activity had been set in motion not only by the

85

crusading effort and the popes' vision of a unified Christendom after the defeat of Islam, but also by the growing political role of the Church in Europe. In the struggle for supremacy the popes relied heavily on the help of the friars as propagandists, collectors of money and trusted agents for diplomatic missions. The members of the two mendicant Orders had access to people of all conditions and were able to keep the pope and the Curia well informed on the situation in the areas to which they were assigned. In the middle of the thirteenth century Franciscans were appointed as papal *nunci* in practically every country in Europe. The delicate task of gathering intelligence and reporting to the Church authorities was carried out brilliantly by the Friars Minor who in this field seem to have displayed greater skill than their Dominican brethren. If the unity and structure of the Church survived intact the profound crisis of this century it was largely thanks to the indefatigable and loyal service of these two Orders.

Teaching the Christian creed and gathering information —these were also the two main tasks assigned by Innocent to the friars sent 'ad Tartaros' in 1245, although at this stage gathering information had perforce priority over the apostolate.

In order to brief the mission adequately, the pope collected all the available reports on the Mongols from Hungary through Berthold, Patriarch of Aquileia. Further information was supplied by a Russian bishop called Peter, about whom very little is known. His report was, however, very accurate on a number of important issues, such as the Mongols' worship of Heaven, their war strategy and the protection they accorded to official envoys. This last item in particular must have had a reassuring effect on Innocent. At the beginning of 1245, he appointed two English Franciscans, John of Stanford and Abraham of Larde, as legates to the Tartars. Shortly after he changed his mind and designated instead John of Pian di Carpine and Lawrence of Portugal. John was to take the land route across eastern Europe, south Russia and Greater Hungary, i.e. the same route followed ten years earlier by Friar Julian, while Lawrence was to reach the Mongols from the Near East. At the same time (March 1245), Innocent also entrusted two Dominican friars with similar missions. They were the Lombard Ascelinus and the French Andrew of Longjumeau, both of whom were instructed to take the route of the Levant.

The pontifical letters carried by these envoys were of several kinds. One, addressed to 'the King and nation of the Tartars', was purely religious in nature. It contained a summary of the Christian teaching couched in biblical language followed by the pontiff's entreaty that the king accept this doctrine. Another letter, also addressed to the Mongol sovereign, was political. In it the pope deprecated the massacres and destructions carried out by the Mongols in Europe, and requested the king to refrain from further attacks. The pope also enquired about his future intentions and hinted at a convenient peace treaty.

These two letters, dated 5 and 13 March respectively, were meant to cover the principal *avowed* aims of the mission, i.e. the establishment of diplomatic relations with the Mongols and the introduction of the Catholic faith among them. The proper use of the letters was, of course, left to the discretion of the bearers. But the mission had, as we have seen, also the more difficult, unofficial task of reporting on all matters concerning the social and military organization of the Mongols. Moreover, the friars were instructed to contact the patriarchs of the schismatic Churches of Russia and Asia Minor, and urge them to rally to the Church of Rome at this critical hour. Innocent, like his predecessor, cherished the hope that the fear of the Mongols would hasten the long-awaited reunion. Therefore the friars were entrusted with a special bull addressed to the leaders of these Churches. In addition to these messages, some of the envoys also carried papal letters for the Ayyubid sultans and princes of Syria, whose territory they had to cross on their way to the Mongols. The letters contained offers of peace, hopes for their conversion and requests of material assistance for the papal ambassadors on their journey.

Almost simultaneously a fifth ambassador, the Franciscan Dominic of Aragon, was sent on an ecclesiastical mission to Armenia and the Greek Church of Byzantium. Apparently the friars who were to take the Near East route had to deliver the papal bulls to the first Mongol chief they met (for transmission to the khaghan) and were not expected to proceed further. Only John of Pian di Carpine had instructions to proceed to the Mongol court if necessary and deliver the letters in person to the emperor.

IV

Friar John, the Diplomat

Sometime between the middle of March and the middle of April 1245 the papal envoys set off in different directions. The mission of Pian di Carpine, who left Lyons on Easter Sunday (16 April), is by far the most interesting and is the best known. His adventurous journey to Mongolia and back lasted two and a half years. His extensive report to the pope, known later under the title of *Ystoria Mongalorum* or *History of the Mongols*, has come down to us in two versions of the thirteenth and fourteenth centuries in numerous manuscript copies. A substantial portion was incorporated in Vincent of Beauvais' encyclopaedic work, the *Speculum Historiale*, completed in 1253. For sheer wealth of information it is matched only by William of Rubruck's account and Marco Polo's *Description of the World*.

Friar John seems to have been born towards the end of the twelfth century. His native place, as we learn from his name, was Pian di Carpine, a small town near Perugia now called Magione. An early disciple of St. Francis, he was sent by him to help establish the Order in Saxony in 1221. He then served in Spain, returning to Germany in 1232 to become Provincial of Saxony. He was very active as a founder of monasteries and schools, and sent friars to most countries in central and northern Europe to introduce or strengthen the Franciscan movement. His friend and con-frère Jordan of Giano (c. 1195–1262) portrays him as a kind, genial and heavily built man, so heavy in fact that he used to ride a donkey instead of the prescribed horse, thereby attracting notice and sympathy wherever he went. He was loved by his brethren for the courage with which he pleaded their causes with princes and bishops, and for watching over them 'as a mother does with her sons, and a hen with her chicks'.

In 1239 he relinquished his post in Saxony and did not reappear in history until 1245, when Innocent chose him as leader of the most important diplomatic mission of the time. Some scholars have suggested that after his departure from Germany he was appointed at the papal court as protonotary, but the evidence is too scanty.

Thus in 1245 Friar John was about sixty years old, and a man who because of his age and physique could hardly be regarded as the ideal candidate for such an arduous mission. Why then was he chosen by the pope for this task? Probably for the following two reasons: Firstly, he was a very experienced and trustworthy man, pious and kind and yet firm, with a good knowledge of languages and of East European affairs. He was, therefore, eminently suited to handle the problem of the reunion of the Russian Church. Furthermore, he was personally acquainted with the King of Bohemia and the Duke of Silesia, two important and useful contacts in these negotiations. Secondly, he was an Italian like the pope. It is only natural that Innocent should have chosen for such a delicate mission a man akin to himself in manners, language and culture.

John was accompanied by Friar Stephen of Bohemia, who later fell ill and had to be left behind. Their trip across Europe took about ten months, that is twice the time that it took them to cross the whole continent of Asia. This was only partly due to poor communications within Europe; much of the delay was caused by lengthy consultations with the leaders of Bohemia, Silesia and Poland, and by the material arrangements for the long journey ahead.

After a stop in Bohemia, where King Wenceslav I, a friend of Friar John, advised the party to proceed by way of Cracow and Kiev, the travellers reached Breslau in Silesia. Here, in the domain of Duke Boleslav II, Friar Benedict the Pole joined the papal embassy. His appointment was prompted by the need for an expert in Slavonic languages, but it is also possible that John felt that Friar Stephen was unlikely to stand the rigours of the journey and so arranged for a replacement.

Until recently Friar Benedict has been regarded as a minor figure in the embassy, although the brief summary of his own report on the journey to the Mongol court, which he dictated in 1247, contains some data not found in John's fuller account. But in 1958 a unique copy of a hitherto unknown version of the friars' travelogue was discovered in most fortuitous circumstances, and was published by Yale University, the present owners of the manuscript. The original was prepared by a certain Friar C. de Bridia on the basis of information supplied mainly by Benedict, to whom we are now indebted for considerable additional material on Mongol history and conquests. Further research on his activity in eastern Europe has also highlighted the part he played in John's attempt to bring about the union of Orthodox Russia with Rome.

Boleslav advised the papal delegation to approach Conrad, Duke of Mazovia and Lanciscia in Poland, who was known to favour the union. Conrad not only played a dominant role in the affairs of the Polish kingdom, but he also exerted a powerful influence, through political and family ties, on the Duchy of Galicia, patrimony of the Russian princes Daniel and Basil Romanovich. As Daniel was the recognized leader of the Russian princes at this time, Innocent was particularly anxious that he should acknowledge the supremacy of the Roman See. It was hoped that such an act on his part would induce the whole of west Russia to join the Catholic anti-Mongol bloc the pope was trying to form.

John, Benedict and Stephen followed Boleslav's advice and went to Cracow to seek Conrad's support and arrange the meeting with the Russian princes and boyars. Benedict, in his capacity as official interpreter of the legation and being himself a Pole, seems to have played a leading part in the negotiations. In Cracow, where they spent several months, the friars had an important conference with Basil (Daniel was then visiting Batu's court), Conrad, and numerous Polish and Hungarian notables. The union with Rome was discussed and the results were so encouraging that Basil invited the pope's legates to Galich (Halicz) for further consultations with the Orthodox bishops and the boyars. The Russian princes were obviously interested in the pope's plan, for this not only gave assurance of future material support against the Mongols, but also guaranteed protection for Galicia from any interference by Poland and Hungary, the other two prominent eastern members of the Catholic bloc. Unfortunately, the former Kievan Russia was now under Mongol jurisdiction and Daniel Romanovich had become in effect a vassal of Batu. A sudden about-face of the Russian princes against the Tartars would at this time have been suicidal. This is why when John and Benedict met the bishops and boyars in Galicia, and asked them to return 'to the unity of Holy Mother Church' they did not get a definite answer. Basil and the notables approved in principle the pope's plan, but decided to wait for Daniel's return before taking a final decision. The friars left Galich for Kiev at the beginning of 1246 convinced that they had succeeded in their first assignment.

During their stay in Cracow our Franciscans had collected more information on the Mongols from Basil and had made preparations to meet them in the appropriate fashion. This included the acquisition of an adequate supply of beaver and badger skins to give away as presents, as it was a strict requirement of Mongol etiquette that envoys should offer expensive gifts to their hosts.

The trip to Kiev, last leg of the European portion of the journey, was undertaken in the heart of the Russian winter and under constant threat from Lithuanian outlaws who were then infesting the region. John and his companions arrived in Kiev safe, but more dead than alive, as the friar himself admits in his report. After a brief halt in the still devastated city, and provided with fresh pack-horses and an escort by the local Mongol 'leader-of-thousand', the party, now comprising about ten people, moved southwards on 3 February.

THE JOURNEY TO BATU AND ACROSS CENTRAL ASIA

About three weeks later, while they were travelling in Coman territory, the friars met the first Mongol camp, where 'some armed Tartars rushed upon us in a horrible manner, wanting to know what kind of men we were.' John and Benedict explained the purpose of their mission and were allowed to proceed, but Stephen who was by now very ill had to be left behind with some of the servants. By this action the envoys complied also with the Mongol practice of keeping some members of a foreign mission as hostages for the period that the mission was in Mongol territory. The Mongols gave them fresh horses and a new escort, and instructed them to proceed to the *ordo*, or camp, of Qurumshi, the nephew of Jochi, who was in command of the whole Coman region. It was at Qurumshi's camp that the friars first became acquainted with the Mongol custom of kneeling three times on the left knee at the entrance of the chief's tent, and of entering without touching the threshold in order to avoid defiling the residence. Qurumshi demanded gifts and sent his visitors to the *ordo* of Batu which was then on the Volga just south of Saratov.

On 4 April the two friars and their escort arrived at Batu's impressive tent city. Here they had to go through more purification rituals, such as passing between two fires, and had to bow to a felt image of Chingis Khan propped up on a cart according to Mongol custom. Received by Batu, an awe-inspiring man then in his forties, they were treated coolly but politely. He had the papal letters translated from Latin into Mongolian (via Russian and Persian), and as these were addressed to the king of the Tartars, he ordered the envoys to carry them personally to the Great Khan Güyüg whose election was about to take place in Mongolia. In the *History of the Mongols* John describes, with a few masterly strokes, the interior of Batu's luxurious linen tent which had formerly belonged to King Béla. Batu sat on a raised platform with his favourite wife, while his brothers, sons and other relatives sat farther down on a bench in the middle of the tent. All the other members of the retinue sat beyond them on the ground, the men on the right and the women on the left. All envoys on their way to the imperial court always took their place on the left, but on their way back they sat on the right. These positions were of great significance to the Mongols as they had been from time immemorial among all the Inner Asian people. They were ultimately related to the movement of the sun, the left corresponding to the east and the rising sun and being, therefore, a more honourable position. Just as in ancient China, where this whole conception probably originated, the central position was the best, hence the Mongol emperor sitting on his throne faced south, and so did, of course, the opening of his tent and the main entrance of the *ordo*. This also applied to the army. The emperor's troops, consisting of his bodyguard and the élite cavalry, were called the Central Army, while the rest of the army was divided into Left and Right Wings. Both in John's *History* and in Rubruck's *Itinerary* we find numerous references to the problem of orientation and ceremonial placing among the Mongols, and from them we can infer how important these were in their society.

In Batu's tent, as in those of all the Mongol princes, food and drink were served in gold and silver vessels, and eating was usually accompanied by singing and music. Our friars unfortunately could not partake of the food because it was the period of Lent and all they had was a plate of gruel. Millet gruel and stewed mutton with broth formed the basic diet of the Mongols.

On Easter Monday (8 April), they left the encampment on the Volga 'with many tears, for we knew not whether we were going to death or to life.'

They were, however, in good hands. As official envoys of a foreign nation they enjoyed a special status which conferred upon them personal immunity and the full use of the official post-relay system. Already in Kiev they had been supplied with Central Asian horses suitable for travel on the wintry steppe—tough horses trained to dig out with their

95

hoofs grass and roots from the soil under the snow. All across Central Asia and Mongolia they rode these wonderfully resilient animals, changing their mounts regularly at the post-stations set up all along the route. The average stage could be up to thirty miles, depending on the distance between water supplies. Passing through deserts they were given stronger horses which could be ridden non-stop for a whole day. In this way they covered a distance of almost three thousand miles in three and a half months. During the latter part of the journey the party had to hasten its pace and ride even at night, as Batu was anxious that they should be present at the election of Güyüg. He obviously wanted them to join the delegations that from all parts of Asia and eastern Europe were congregating at the Mongol court to pay homage to the new emperor.

The route followed by the friars after they left Batu's camp crossed the country of the Kangli Turks north of the Aral Sea and, following the Syr Darya, passed through the towns of Yanikant (near modern Kazalinsk in Kazakhstan), Barchin (near Kizil Orda) and Otrar. From northern Khorezm, whose desolate waste was a silent testimony to the recent invasion, they moved into the old Qara-Khitai territory south of the Balkash. The party crossed the Chu, Ili and Emil rivers in June. Then, through Omyl (now Tacheng in Sinkiang), and by way of Lake Ulyungur and the river Urungu, they reached the Altai mountains, which they crossed probably at the Dabistan Daban Pass at the end of June. In this way, from Dzungaria they entered into the former Naiman country in western Mongolia, that is, broadly speaking, the region between Kobdo and Uliasutai. From there they proceeded due east, crossed the Khangai range and arrived at Güyüg's *ordo* near Karakorum on 22 July.

During this long and, for the time, unusually fast journey across Asia, our travellers had to bear intense physical discomforts. Friar John, in particular, being a heavy man, must have found riding on the small Mongolian horses for weeks on end a very trying experience. They had to contend also with extreme climatic conditions, from the searing heat and dryness of the desert to the rigours of the Altai, often with only one meal a day. These difficulties did not prevent the two friars from making mental observations about the country and the inhabitants they met, noting all the scraps of information they could gather from the local people and their own guides. We must not forget that John and Benedict were the first Western explorers of this immense *terra incognita*. Their observations, accurate when based on personal experience, are of course less reliable when they concern other regions of Asia about which they learned only indirectly. In their narratives we find the names of many well-known peoples inhabiting the lands which they crossed, such as the Comans, Alans, Khazars, Kangli, Black Kitayans (i.e. the Qara-Khitai), and the Naimans. But then we read in John's *History* that 'after the Samoyedes are those men who are said to have faces like dogs and live in the wilderness along the shores of the oceans.' In Benedict's account these remote inhabitants of northern Asia are actually called 'the dog-headed Cynocephali'. The Parossites, who are mentioned immediately after the Samoyedes, are described by Benedict as people having such narrow mouths that they cannot eat any solid food, and inhale instead the steam of cooking meat and fruit. Here, as in several other instances, the description of peoples and places is enriched with information drawn from Western geographical lore. The Cynocephali we have already encountered. As for the people living on steam, the legend is found in Pliny's description of an Indian tribe. This tendency to mingle fact and fable is not peculiar to our authors, but it is a common trait of all medieval travellers steeped in the cultural tradition of the Bible and the Alexander Romance.

AT THE MONGOL COURT

Although John and Benedict are the first Western authors to mention Karakorum, they did not actually visit it. The great assembly that elected Güyüg was held about half a day's ride south of the Mongol capital. In this place a huge tent city had been erected to accommodate the thousands of Mongol nobles and officers, and the foreign envoys with their retinues. The ceiling of the imperial tent was of gold-embroidered cloth, hence the name of *Shira Ordo* or Yellow Camp given to this temporary court.

In his *History of the World-Conqueror* the contemporary Persian historian Juvaini (?1226–83) lists the principal delegations present at the enthronement, among them the 'envoys from the Franks'. There is hardly any doubt that the envoys in question were our Franciscans, since the term 'Frank' was then the current designation in Asia for any Western European. Among the other envoys from Europe was Alexander Nevsky's father, the Grand Duke Iaroslav, who never returned to Russia. He died at the Mongol camp, his body, as John describes it, turning 'strangely bluish'. This led the friars to conclude that he had been poisoned by order of the notorious dowager Töregene, which is quite unlikely.

From Georgia came David IV, son of Queen Rusudan, and David V, the illegitimate son of her brother, King George, while King Hethum I (1226–69) of Lesser Armenia (Cilicia) was represented by his brother Prince Sempad.

Sultans, emirs, atabegs and cadis from Syria, Iraq and Turkestan came to bring tribute and make obeisance to the Mongol ruler. John also mentions the envoy of the Caliph of Baghdad and the 'great chiefs' of Kitai (north China) and Solangi (Korea).

All the Mongol aristocracy was present except Batu who, as we have mentioned earlier, had opposed the election of Güyüg from the beginning. Since Güyüg's mother, Töregene, had eventually succeeded in gaining the support of the majority of the princes for her son, Batu preferred to dissociate himself from the election, thus infringing one of the major rules of the Mongol code and widening further the rift within the royal family.

The friars were lodged in better quarters than those assigned to the other ambassadors, probably because they were envoys of a Western leader whose country was not tributary to the Mongols and whose intentions were not yet known. Significantly they were not required to genuflect with all the others when Güyüg, at the end of the colourful ceremonies of the election, was placed on the golden throne by the princes and the nobility. The great event took place on 24 August 1246 at a place three or four leagues from the *Shira Ordo*. The date of the enthronement had actually been fixed for a few days earlier, but there had been a great hailstorm on 15 August, and this was regarded as a bad omen by the shamans and diviners. The ceremony was postponed and the place had to be changed. Violent hail and thunderstorms, and even snowfalls, in the middle of summer are not uncommon phenomena in Mongolia, but the medieval Mongols were positively awed by them. Their ancestral fear of natural forces partly explains the large number of astrologers and fortune-tellers in the imperial entourage.

The barbarian splendour of the court and the ceremonies

accompanying Güyüg's enthronement are vividly described by Friar John who, as a medieval man, was naturally very interested in them. He and Benedict watched the gathering and procession of nobles clad in bright coloured robes, the colour changing each day for four successive days. They had to take part in the wild drinking and eating that preceded and followed the enthronement, doing their best to restrain themselves and avoid the inebriating kumys without offending their hosts. They admired the immense wealth of silk, brocade, furs and gems brought as tribute to Güyüg from all over Asia, and his gold and ivory throne, encrusted with pearls and jewels, made by the Russian goldsmith Cosmas. This artist, who had also carved the imperial seal, became a friend of the friars and it was from him that they gained most of their knowledge about Tartar affairs and customs. The two papal legates had no gifts to offer to the new emperor as they had been forced to yield all of them to Qurumshi, Batu and other rapacious Mongol officers met on the journey.

As it was customary, after the election Güyüg had to attend to family business, rewarding his supporters and disposing of those relatives and officials whom he regarded as potential enemies. The two main victims of the purge were his own uncle and a lady of Töregene's entourage, called Fatima, who was accused of witchcraft. Both were executed, the lady, as Juvaini informs us, by being cast into the river after having had all her orifices sewn up and been rolled in a sheet of felt. Abominable practices such as this, and the slow crushing to death under wooden planks to which the unfortunate Mstislav of Kiev was subjected after the battle on the Kalka, were not enforced out of sheer cruelty as some authors claim. Their rationale is rather to be found in the shamanistic belief that blood contains the soul or spiritual essence of man, and that when a noble's blood was spilt, it exerted a malign influence on the ground on which it fell. It was, indeed, a mark of distinction for an enemy to be executed by suffocation, usually by being rolled up in carpets, as this was the form of death regularly used for members of the khan's family. Both Mstislav and Fatima were actually treated as special victims—an honour with which they would have gladly dispensed!

At the same time Güyüg reinstated some of the former ministers of Ögödei who had been earlier persecuted by his mother. One of them, the Nestorian Chinqai, was re-appointed as chief secretary, 'protonotary', as John calls him. It was he who arranged the interview of the papal legates with the Great Khan and who, afterwards, drafted the latter's reply to the pontiff.

Güyüg had already been informed by Batu's messengers of the contents of the pope's letters. He was surprised and disappointed that the representatives of such an exalted person as the pope should have come to him empty-handed. After his enthronement he showed his disappointment by reducing their food rations. The two friars would have starved had they not been providentially helped by the goldsmith Cosmas. They had, nevertheless, several inter-views with the emperor to whom they conveyed again, in writing and through interpreters, the pope's wishes and expectations. During these meetings they had ample oppor-tunity to observe the world's most powerful and feared leader at close quarters. He was, writes John, 'forty or forty-five years old or more, of medium height, very intelligent and extremely shrewd, and most grave in his manners.' The unsmiling lord of the Tartars was actually a sick, prematurely old man, used up by alcohol and women. He was only forty at the time and doomed to die less than two years later.

When the time arrived for Güyüg to reply to Innocent's letters, the emperor enquired whether the pope had people who could read Russian, Persian and Mongolian. Friar John replied that these languages were not used in the country where he came from, and suggested instead that the reply be first written in Mongolian and then be explained to him in detail by the court secretaries, so that he and Benedict could prepare a faithful version in Latin. His suggestion was followed and on 11 November Chinqai and another scribe translated Güyüg's reply word by word, making sure that the friars' rendering into Latin was accurate. Two days later, when John and Benedict were about to leave, the secretaries gave them also a version of the reply in Persian duly stamped with the imperial seal. Güyüg, moreover, proposed sending his own envoys to the pope, but John, fearing that they might report back to the emperor on the internal discords and weakness of Europe, objected to this plan on various grounds and succeeded in deferring it. As a final act of courtesy they paid a call on Güyüg's mother, Töregene, who in return gave each of them as a parting gift a fur cloak and a length of velvet.

Güyüg's Reply and Friar John's Report

The party, comprising as before the two friars, their servant and a Mongol escort, set out on the long return journey, travelling by the same route across Asia through the winter. It must have been rather a sad journey for the two Franciscans. Güyüg's reply bode ill for Christianity and for Europe. It was a rebuff to the pope and an order to acknowledge immediately Mongol supremacy. The Latin version of the reply is found in Benedict's short account and is also recorded more fully by the chronicler Salimbene of Adam

(1221–88?), who copied it directly from John's original after the latter's return. The Persian version is still extant in the Secret Archives of the Vatican. It was first published by the French savant Paul Pelliot in 1923 (for a new translation see the Appendix). Of the two, the Latin version is much closer to the lost Mongol original.

In his letter, Güyüg enjoins the pope and the kings of Europe to come together to the Mongol court to pay homage and receive his commands. He then proceeds to deal with the issues raised in the papal letters. He claims that he fails to understand the pope's request that he should accept baptism, and expresses surprise at his comment concerning the fate of the Hungarians and the other Christian people attacked by the Mongols. Have they not disobeyed the order of Heaven as conveyed to them by Chingis Khan and Ögödei and did they not kill the Mongol envoys? Güyüg argues that the mere fact that these people were destroyed shows that this was the will of God. He accuses the pope of arrogance when the latter claims, in his letter, that his is the only true Christianity. Here Güyüg is referring to the Nestorians whose clergy he and his family especially favoured. Several of his chancellors belonged also to this faith, and it was Chinqai who, in all likelihood, had drafted the text of Güyüg's reply. 'How dost thou know whom God forgives, to whom He shows mercy?' asks the Great Khan reproachfully. Güyüg goes on pointing out that the whole world from sunset to sunrise has been granted to the Mongol ruler by the power of Heaven; how can such a thing be achieved unless it were willed by Him? He again urges the pope and kings of Europe to submit and offer their services to him. Should they disobey the command, God alone knows what would befall them!

The threat implied in the last sentence is perfectly clear

and it is further emphasized by the legend on the letter's seal, which reads: 'By the strength of Eternal Heaven, Order of the Universal Ruler of the Empire of the Great Mongols. When it reaches the subject and the rebel people, let them respect it, let them fear it!' The meaning of the legend had already been explained to John by the seal's maker, Cosmas. From conversations with him and with several other Russian and Hungarian captives whom they met at the *Shira Ordo*, the friars had also learned about the emperor's political ambitions. The letter only confirmed what they had found out privately, namely that the Mongols now firmly believed that the whole world should submit to them as this was the will of Heaven.

Now in China the theory that the founder of a new dynasty possesses the Mandate of Heaven had been accepted for over two thousand years. The traditional Chinese conception held that the unmistakable proof that a leader possessed the Mandate was the success that followed his bid to seize the throne from the ruling dynasty. We know that this pragmatic view was propounded by the Chinese advisers of Chingis Khan and Ögödei, and it seems that it may also have influenced through them the world-conception of the Mongol emperors. The lip service paid to the khans by the representatives of Islam, Buddhism, Taoism and Nestorian Christianity must have also enhanced their feeling of superiority and strengthened the belief in their divine mission. Gradually they came to conceive the world as the Mongol empire-in-the-making, whose leaders by Heavenly appointment were Chingis Khan's successors. Even though many nations were still outside the Great Khan's control, they were nevertheless regarded as potential members of this universal Mongol empire. It followed that the people who had not yet brought tribute and offered submission to the Mongol court were considered also as rebels to this divinely inspired social order. For the Mongols war against these nations was, therefore, right and necessary, just as the medieval crusades against the heretics were right and necessary in the eyes of contemporary Christians.

It is in the light of this doctrine that one must understand the language of Güyüg's letter and the Mongol attitude towards international relations as expressed in all their diplomatic correspondence with the Western nations. Until this attitude changed no dialogue was possible between East and West. So much was clear to Friar John who, in his narrative, remarks: 'It is the intention of the Tartars to bring the whole world into subjection if they can and . . . on this point they have received a command from Chingiscan. . . . This also accounts for their refusing to make peace with any nation unless, as has been told, they surrender into their hands.'

Thus, there was only one course of action left for Christian Europe: to prepare for war. It was chiefly with this consideration in mind that John on his return journey began preparing his report to the pope. This took the form of a description of the Mongols and the way to deal with them. The account was divided into sections dealing with all the important aspects of Mongol life. It begins with a concise description of the land of the Tartars and its climate. This is followed by chapters devoted to the people, their religion and customs, Mongol history, warfare and the countries conquered by them. In his survey of Mongol society the Franciscan monk shows an amazing realism and impartiality. He seems to have captured the minutest details of life at the Mongol camp. Due recognition is given to the Mongols' virtues, such as the respect they show towards their elders, their discipline in war, their honesty among themselves and the chastity of their women. Their vices are, likewise, amply described, among the obvious ones, their cruelty and treachery towards their enemies, repellent personal habits and insatiable greed for material goods. Among their social customs levirate is illustrated by John with the example of the brother of Andrew, Duke of Chernigov, who was forced by Batu to marry Andrew's widow: 'She replied that she preferred to be killed than break her law. But Bati [i.e. Batu] nevertheless gave her to him as wife, although both of them refused as much as they could. And they put them to bed together and placed the youth on top of her in spite of her tears and cries, and forced them to unite.'

The Tartars' military skill and religious beliefs, both particularly relevant to John's mission, received special treatment. Thus the Western world was given for the first time a comprehensive picture of the Mongols' rigid military code, the decimal organization of their army, their weapons and equipment, and their fighting techniques both in open combat and in attacking fortifications.

In dealing with their religious practices John had to confine himself to the outward manifestations. His description of the making and cult of felt idols, the role of the shamans in society, and the Mongols' purification and burial customs is especially valuable, as many of these practices survived until only a generation or two ago among certain tribes of Central Asia and Siberia. Among them we may mention the horse sacrifice, and the curious practice of sticking the straw-filled skin of a horse on poles above the grave of the deceased. Until recent times the ancestral idols made of felt, known as *ongot*, were a common feature of the Mongolian *ger* or tent house.

One of the most interesting sections is that devoted to the origin of the Mongol empire, as it shows a further elaboration of the Prester John legends and the Chingis Romance. In John's account and in Benedict's own narrative, Chingis Khan is no longer identified with Prester John or King David, but appears in his true light as pagan founder of the Mongol power. Prester John is mentioned as the Christian king of Greater India, i.e. the Indian subcontinent between the Indus and the Ganges, who defeated Chingis Khan's army with a stratagem involving metal dummies and Greek fire. The story is reminiscent of the legendary account of Alexander's defeat of the Indian king Porus, whose elephants were routed by the Macedonian's soldiers using red-hot bronze statues filled with burning embers and placed on iron carts. However, John's account also reflects current stories about the Mongols' well-known use of manikins and incendiaries in their campaigns, and the defeat of one of their generals by the Khorezmians in 1221.

The fictional and semi-fictional material included in the friars' reports derives largely from stories about Chingis Khan which circulated in Asia at the time. These stories blended themes from the Oriental versions of the Alexander Romance, the Prester John legend and factual accounts of Chingis Khan's exploits. The Mongols themselves must have contributed to the development of the Chingis Romance by embroidering upon the conqueror's epic life, episodes of which were told and retold around the camp fires. Contamination with the Alexander Romance was easy, as the Mongols were also acquainted with it. A thirteenth- or fourteenth-century Mongolian version of the Romance came to light only a few years ago. As for the tales about the defeats suffered by Chingis Khan and his generals, clearly meant to ridicule and spite the Mongols, they were picked up by the friars from foreign captives, especially Russians, who had every reason to hate their masters.

With the exception of these stories, and of occasional references to Cynocephali, Monopodes and other monsters, usually relegated to the Arctic region and inaccessible deserts, Friar John's report is free of mythological elements and marvels.

In the case of the Kitai or Chinese, of whom John gives the first Western account, we again have a curious blend of fact and fiction. Innocent's envoys must have seen quite a few Chinese at the *Shira Ordo*, and John gives a brief but accurate description of their physique (lack of beard, resemblance to the Mongols, but not so broad in the face), their superb skill as craftsmen, their peculiar script and their affability and kindness. At the same time, he relates that 'they also have, so it seems, an Old and New Testament, and lives of Fathers and hermits, and buildings made like churches, in which they pray at stated times; and they say they have some saints. They worship one God, they honour Our Lord Jesus Christ, and they believe in eternal life, but are not baptized. They show honour and respect to our Scriptures, they love Christians and give much in alms.' John's statement that the Chinese honoured Jesus and loved Christians is of course not true. He almost certainly got this information from some Nestorians at the Mongol court who distorted the facts. Nestorian Christianity had virtually disappeared in China after the middle of the ninth century. It is true that it returned to China in the twelfth and thirteenth centuries, but its followers were mainly found among foreigners, i.e. non-Chinese, who came in the wake of the barbarian conquerors. By 'Old and New Testament' are probably meant the Chinese Canonical Books and the Classics, which embody the works of the Confucian school. Although these errors can be explained, the fact remains that John's picture of China is an idealistic one. The Chinese are humane, industrious and civilized people, and all they need to be perfect Christians is baptism. This image is strongly reminiscent of the classical image of the Seres with which John as a learned man was no doubt acquainted.

During their stay among the Mongols the friars realized that any effort to convert their hosts to Christianity would have been premature, and it is doubtful whether they even made any attempt in this direction. John apparently took advantage of the fatal illness of Duke Iaroslav to convert him to Catholicism, but this event is known to us only indirectly and is questionable. Disappointed with the poor results of his religious mission, our Franciscan found consolation in the thought that China at least promised to be an ideal land for missionary work.

As for the Mongols, nothing but violence could be expected from them. Hence the important eighth chapter on 'How to wage war against the Tartars', which is really the culmination of John's discourse. The technical aspect of defence, such as the organization of the Western forces on the model of the Mongol army, is a thorough and ingenious piece of military writing. However, the essence of his advice is the union of all Christian nations: 'Therefore, if Christians wish to save themselves, their country and Christendom, then kings, princes, barons and rulers of countries ought to assemble together and by common consent send men to fight against the Tartars before they begin to spread over the land.'

The elaboration and summing up of their experiences must have kept the two friars busy during the long return journey. They followed the same route back to Batu's camp, but as this time they were travelling in winter they had to contend with snow, blizzards, and more hardship. Batu, whose camp they reached on the day of the Ascension

(9 May 1247), gave them a safe conduct to cross his territory. On the way to Kiev the friars collected Stephen and the servants left behind with him.

The party arrived in Kiev on 9 June, sixteen months after they had left the Russian city, and were congratulated by the local people as if they had come back from the dead. Daniel and Basil Romanovich entertained them lavishly for a whole week, quite against their will, and before the friars resumed their journey the two brothers declared their wish to join the Church of Rome, an ephemeral promise which later events showed had been made solely with the aim of obtaining military assistance from the pope.

On their way to Cologne and Lyons, the travellers passed through Poland and Hungary. They met King Béla and informed him of the outcome of their mission. Their account confirmed what Béla had already learned from his own emissaries, namely that the Tartars intended to return and conquer the rest of Europe. These and subsequent reports prompted the Hungarian monarch to seek a *modus vivendi* with the Mongols in order to avert a further devastation of his country. From previous experience he had learned that his friends and allies could not be relied upon for assistance at a time of crisis. The marriage of his son Stephen (later King Stephen V) to a Coman princess shortly after these events was determined by Béla's new policy of appeasement.

On 3 October the friars arrived in Cologne and it was in this city that Benedict dictated his own report of the journey. On 18 November they were back in Lyons, where Pope Innocent was anxiously awaiting them. John and Benedict gave the pontiff a full account of their mission and delivered the letters of Güyüg and Daniel to him. John's report was revised and put into final form. Friar Salimbene of Adam, who met him near Lyons at the beginning of November, records in his chronicle how John used to have his 'great book about the deeds of the Tattars' read aloud by those who were interested in his experiences, and how he would explain all things in detail to the astonished readers. Incidentally, John pointed out to Salimbene that 'Tattar' and not 'Tartar' was the correct form of the name, but his remarks did not affect the current usage of this term in western Europe.

It seems, however, that there were already some people who, not surprisingly, questioned the truth of John's account of the Mongols. To counter the accusation of being a liar, John wrote a final chapter, in which he mentioned the places visited by the papal embassy and the people met on the way, including the Venetian and Genoese merchants encountered in Russia.

According to Salimbene, the pope was very pleased with the report, even though the outcome of the mission was not really what he had hoped. Soon after he entrusted the energetic friar with another delicate mission, this time to King Louis of France, to which we shall return later. Upon completion of this mission Innocent made him Archbishop of Antivari in Dalmatia. Friar John died in Italy, probably at Perugia, in 1252.

V

The Dominican Envoys

John of Pian di Carpine was not the first of the papal envoys sent in 1245 to return to Lyons. The Minorite Dominic of Aragon had come back in April 1247, and at about the same time, or shortly after, the Dominican Andrew of Longjumeau had also returned from the Near East.

The outcome of Dominic's mission is not known, but it appears that he had no contact with the Mongols and that his diplomatic activity, directed mainly to the reunion of the Churches, was confined to Syria, Little Armenia and Constantinople.

The mission of Andrew of Longjumeau* is, on the other hand, better known. After his arrival in the Holy Land Andrew, accompanied by a friar of his own order, had crossed the domains of the sultans of Baalbek and Homs in Syria, and tried to obtain the latter's assistance in reaching the Mongol outposts. The sultan, suspecting a collusion between the pope and the Mongols, was not very helpful. Andrew and his companion then slowly made their way to Mosul in northern Mesopotamia, which was already under Mongol control, and from there they eventually reached the province of Tabriz in Greater Armenia. This region had been taken over by the Mongol general Chormaghan who, as we have

* A small town in France, between Paris and Melun.

seen earlier, had been sent by Ögödei to reconquer Khorezm. Between 1231 and 1239 he had become master of north-western Persia, as well as of the whole territory between Tiflis in Georgia and Tabriz. He had been replaced in 1242 by Baiju, a commander appointed by the regent Töregene. Baiju (1242–56) conquered the Seljuk kingdom of Konya (Iconium) which bordered on the Byzantine empire, and extended Mongol control over Lesser Armenia and northern Mesopotamia. Although ruthless towards the local popula-tion, the Mongol military chiefs had accorded protection to the Nestorian communities of these countries. In 1235 Ögödei had appointed a Syrian cleric called Simeon Rabban-ata as leader of the Nestorian Christians with headquarters at Tabriz. With Chormaghan's protection, Simeon had built many churches and spread his influence over the whole territory occupied by the Mongols. He had retained his position under Baiju, although the new commander was less favourable to the Christians than his predecessor.

It was on their way to Baiju's camp, and almost certainly at Tabriz, that Andrew of Longjumeau met the Nestorian pre-late to whom he delivered the papal bulls addressed to the schismatic Churches. Simeon replied with a letter for the pope in which he openly professed allegiance to the Apostolic See.

Proceeding farther in the region of Tabriz, the Dominican envoy met a Mongol army detachment and handed the two papal letters for the king of the Tartars to the officer in charge. The friars then turned westwards and reached Antioch. There they met Ignatius II, Patriarch of the Jaco-bite Christians, who like Simeon replied to the pontiff in terms favourable to the union of the Churches.

Andrew's mission had failed to establish direct contact with the commander-in-chief of the Mongol forces in Asia Minor, but together with the letters from the Nestorians, the

Jacobites and the Sultan of Syria, the Dominicans brought back useful information collected on the journey. In the summary of his report on the Tartars that has been preserved in Matthew Paris's *Chronica Majora* Andrew mentions the Mongol emperor's ambition to conquer the world, and the organization and strength of his armies. There is also a reference to the Prester John legend in the version given to him by Simeon, according to which Chingis Khan had slain Prester John, King of India, and married his daughter. A fuller version of the same story, apparently told by the same Simeon to Friar Ascelinus a few months later, substitutes for Prester John 'his son David', and places the event in 1202. The story is interesting because it shows that in Nestorian circles the figure of the last 'real' Prester John or King David, i.e. the Naiman prince Küchlüg, had already merged with that of Toghril, the Nestorian Ong-khan of the Kereits, who had been defeated by Chingis Khan in 1203. In actual fact, a niece of Toghril, not a daughter, had been married to Chingis; however, a daughter of the Ong-khan had been sought by Chingis for his eldest son Jochi in 1202–3. This request had been rejected, and soon after Chingis had fallen out with the Kereits. The Nestorian version, which combined the two events, must have been circulating in Asia for several decades as there is a faint echo of it in Friar Julian's report, and traces can be found even in one of the versions of the famous *Report on King David* of about 1220.

If the letters brought back from Andrew were encouraging so far as the schismatic Christians were concerned, they were less so with regard to the Moslem princes. The Christian Churches of Asia Minor, caught between the hostile Moslem population and the oppressive and unpredictable Mongols, were eager to respond to the pope's appeal for Christian unity. In contrast to this, the guarded replies of the sultans of Syria indicated that while they were aware of the Tartar danger, they were also suspicious of Innocent's motives behind his offer of peace. In his letters and through his envoys the pope must have made it clear that the emperor Frederick would be excluded from any future negotiations. This attitude was bound to provoke the antagonism of those sultans who were Frederick's personal friends. Moreover, the eagerness with which Innocent sought to establish contact with the Mongols could not fail to rouse the suspicion that he was trying to establish a secret alliance with them against the Turks. This was certainly not the case then, but later events proved that the danger of such an alliance for the Moslem world was very real indeed.

As for the papal letters to the Mongol emperor which Andrew handed over to the Mongol commander near Tabriz, they do not seem to have ever reached either Baiju or the Mongol court. Their fate is unknown.

THE MISSION OF FRIAR ASCELINUS

The last of the missions 'ad Tartaros' to report to the pope in Lyons was that of the Dominican Ascelinus whose return must be placed between July and September 1248. The story of this embassy is known to us through an interesting account left by one of its members, Simon of St. Quentin, much of which was later incorporated in Vincent of Beauvais' *Speculum Historiale*. Simon's report, although inferior to that of John of Pian di Carpine, is also important for the information it contains on conditions in Georgia and Armenia.

Ascelinus, like Andrew of Longjumeau, took the route of the Levant. He and his three companions, collected from Dominican friaries on the way, wandered for a considerable time in Palestine and Syria trying, like Andrew, to gain access to the Mongols through the Moslem principalities. Their movements are not very clear, but it appears that they failed in their attempt to cross the Syrian desert and turned instead northwards, reaching Tiflis in Georgia through Antioch, Cilicia and Greater Armenia. In Tiflis they chose another companion from the local Dominican monastery who was acquainted with Mongol customs. The party then proceeded to Baiju's summer camp, situated at Sisian in the Karabakh Highland, northeast of present Nakhichevan in the South Armenian Republic.

The Dominicans arrived at the Mongol encampment on 24 May 1247, well over two years after leaving France. Ascelinus's interview with Baiju began, almost literally, on the wrong foot. Requested to make the triple genuflexion when he was introduced to his presence, the proud friar and his companions obstinately refused. This already serious breach of etiquette was made even worse by Ascelinus's failure to bring the customary presents, by his referring to the pope as 'the greatest of all men', and by his demanding that Baiju and the Mongols become Christian. To this, one of the nobles in Baiju's entourage replied: 'You ask us to become Christians and so dogs just like you! Isn't your pope a dog and aren't all you Christians dogs?' Baiju, enraged, issued a sentence of death against the envoys. Others suggested some exemplary punishment to warn the pope, such as flaying Ascelinus alive and sending his straw-filled skin to his masters. The timely intervention of one of Baiju's wives and the remonstrances of the officer in charge of the friars, who invoked the law protecting official envoys, saved the lives of the Dominicans. Baiju then ordered that the friars should go to Karakorum to deliver the papal letters and see in person 'the power and glory of the Great Khan'. Ascelinus, having been instructed to hand the letters to the first Mongol chief he met, flatly refused. The inflexible position assumed by the friars forced Baiju to accept the letters and forward them to the Mongol capital. The two bulls, translated from Latin into Persian by the Greek and Turkish interpreters of Baiju and then rendered into Mongolian, were sent by special messenger to Karakorum. Ascelinus requested also a reply from Baiju himself, but the commander showed little inclination to comply and kept the friars waiting for several weeks, still debating whether to execute them or not. The arrival at his camp of a high Mongol official from Karakorum settled the question. The official, Eljigidei by name, knew of John of Pian di Carpine's mission and was also acquainted with Güyüg's reply to the pope. He was, moreover, the carrier of an imperial edict which Mongol military leaders were to issue to representatives of all foreign countries.

After due consultations with Eljigidei, Baiju finally issued the friars with two documents. One was his own reply to the pope's letters, couched in terms very similar to those of Güyüg's letter and clearly inspired by it; the other was the Great Khan's edict carried by Eljigidei. This was simply a reaffirmation of the supreme authority of the Mongol emperor, and a warning to all those nations that dared transgress his orders. The document restated what Güyüg had said to Friar John eight months earlier, namely that the pope should recognize himself as vassal of the Mongols if he wished to avoid the destruction of his domains.

Two envoys chosen by Baiju, one a Turk and the other a Nestorian Syrian, were ordered to accompany the papal embassy and bring back the pope's reply. These envoys, the first 'Mongol' ambassadors to the West, were no doubt also instructed to gain a first-hand knowledge of the situation in Europe. The party left the Mongol camp on 25 July, exactly nine weeks after the Dominicans' arrival.

On the way back Ascelinus and his companions took the southern route. At Tabriz, where they stopped a few days, they met Simeon Rabban-ata who, this time, showed little friendliness towards the ambassadors of the pope, perhaps on account of reports he may have received of the friars' behaviour at Baiju's camp. On the other hand, Ascelinus may have also annoyed the Nestorian cleric with his lack of tact and rather overbearing manners.

The Dominicans took the road to Mosul and thence, through Aleppo and Antioch, reached Acre. They lingered in Palestine for several months before sailing for Europe and were not back in Lyons until the late summer of 1248. Matthew Paris records in his chronicle the arrival of the Mongol envoys and the extreme secrecy which surrounded the purpose of their mission. Eventually, on 22 November, Innocent gave the two envoys his written reply to Baiju. In his letter the pontiff urged the Mongols to stop persevering in their errors and to end the slaughter, especially of Christians. There is not even a hint at a renewal of the dialogue with the Tartars. The papal missions may have been successful in collecting information on the Mongols, but they had not achieved their political and religious aims. There was, simply, no way of bridging the politico-religious ideology of the Mongols and that of the Church, both claiming to be universal and divinely inspired. Innocent, who had by now received all the reports from his envoys,* recognized the impasse and rightly felt that at this stage there was no point in pushing the negotiations further.

The temporary suspension of the Church's diplomatic activity with the Mongol court opened a new chapter in the relations between Christian Europe and the Tartars, and

---

* Nothing is known about the outcome of Lawrence of Portugal's mission and it is not even certain whether it ever reached the Near East.

one in which a leading part was played by King Louis IX of France.

THE SECOND MISSION OF ANDREW OF LONGJUMEAU

The highlight of the First General Council of Lyons (28 June–18 July 1245) convoked by Innocent IV was the deposition of Frederick II, whom the pope, the bishops and the rulers of Europe found guilty of heresy, perjury and failure to heed his original excommunication. The other resolutions of the Council included a call for a new Crusade, for help to the people of western Europe threatened by the Mongols, and for negotiations with the Greeks to end the Eastern Schism. The 'Tartar peril' was, together with Frederick's treachery, the dominant theme of the Council, and both the resolutions concerning eastern Europe and the Oriental Churches were largely motivated by it.

With regard to the Crusade against the Moslems, there was no need to look for a leader as one was at hand already and more than willing to take the Cross. This was Louis IX, the young and deeply religious king of France, who in the course of a serious illness in 1244 had vowed to set out for a Crusade. The pope had merely to confirm Louis's vows and arrange for the Crusade to be preached throughout France. Louis got meagre support from the other monarchs of Europe, and his Crusade, the Seventh, was a purely French affair. The preparations took three years, during which the war between Innocent and the deposed emperor in Italy reached unparalleled violence. At the beginning of 1248 the situation was so critical that the pope sent John of Pian di Carpine as his secret envoy to Louis, to urge the king to postpone his journey to the Holy Land and join instead the papal armies in the Crusade against Frederick. Louis, however, stood firm in his resolution and on 25 August the French Crusaders, led by the king and by Queen Margaret, sailed from Aigues-Mortes for Cyprus.

On 17 September the royal squadron anchored at Limassol. The next six months were spent on the island making plans and organizing the campaign against Egypt. It was during his stay at Nicosia, on 20 December, that Louis received the visit of two emissaries from the Mongols. Their names were David and Mark, they were both Nestorian Christians from Mosul, and they carried a letter from Eljigidei. The message, written in Persian, was translated for the king of France by the Dominican friar Andrew of Longjumeau who was then in Louis's entourage and who, apparently, had already met one of the envoys at the Mongol camp near Tabriz in early 1247.

The content of the letter, which has survived only in its Latin version, is very interesting. Eljigidei prays God for the success of the Christian forces against the enemies of the Cross. He claims to have been sent by Güyüg to protect the Christians and rebuild their churches, and affirms that Latins, Greeks, Armenians, Nestorians, Jacobites and all worshippers of the Cross are one in the eyes of God and the Mongol emperor. The letter refers also to an oral message carried by the two envoys which the king of France should heed. This message did indeed clarify the purpose of the letter. Eljigidei, the envoys said, had been appointed by Güyüg supreme commander of the Mongol forces in Western Asia. As he was planning to lay siege to Baghdad the following spring, he hoped that the Franks would carry out a simultaneous attack on Egypt and, in this way, prevent the sultan from coming to the aid of the Caliph. The two emissaries made the proposal sound more attractive by adding that Güyüg's mother was the daughter of Prester John, that both Eljigidei and Güyüg had been converted to Christianity, and that they intended to help the Christians to free Jerusalem. It is impossible to say whether these stories were fabricated by the envoys eager to ensure the success of their mission, or whether they had been instructed to relate them by the cunning Eljigidei. The Mongol commander's scheme was ingenious. The Caliphate was the last strong political power in the Near East, and the Mongols, having strengthened their position in Persia and Asia Minor, were now ready to come to grips with it. Eljigidei had evidently heard of Louis's plan to reconquer Jerusalem and of his impending departure for the Near East. We know from Simon of St. Quentin that Ascelinus was closely questioned in the Mongol camp about rumours of a Frankish invasion of Syria that were circulating at the time. Eljigidei was quick to see the advantages that would derive from a Mongol-Frankish military alliance. Predictably, his offer, combined with the unexpected news of Güyüg's conversion, roused wild hopes at the court in Nicosia. Louis saw in these developments a confirmation of independent reports that he had received shortly before from Armenian sources emphasizing the influence of the Christian element at the Mongol court. He immediately notified the pope and set about preparing a suitable reply. This took the form of letters to Eljigidei and Güyüg in which the king warmly commended their attitude towards Christianity. To further show his appreciation, Louis, following the envoys' advice, had a beautiful portable chapel made of scarlet and in the shape of a tent. This richly decorated chapel, complete with all the paraphernalia for the celebration of the Mass, and some fragments of the True Cross, were the main royal gifts for the Great Khan. The Frankish embassy appointed by Louis to accompany the envoys back to Eljigidei's camp and carry the letters and the presents to the Mongol emperor was

led again by Andrew of Longjumeau, whose previous experience and knowledge of Oriental languages made him an
obvious choice. He was, presumably, also entrusted by Louis
with an oral message for Eljigidei concerning his intention of
collaborating with the Mongols against the Moslems.

The seven-man embassy, which besides Andrew comprised
his brother William (also a Dominican), a third friar, clerks
and guards, left Nicosia for Antioch on 27 January 1249.
With them went, of course, the two envoys. As in the earlier
journey Andrew entered the Mongol-occupied territory
through Mosul. Some time in the spring he and his companions reached the encampment of Eljigidei in the region
of Tabriz. By then, however, the situation had changed again
and they met with a different reception from the one they
expected. In the lapse of time between the departure of
David and Mark and the arrival of Andrew several momentous events had occurred in the Mongol world. Güyüg had
died (March–April 1248) and his widow, Oghul Qaimish,
had become regent of the empire. A woman of Töregene's
stamp, she forcefully tried to rally support for her son by
Güyüg, against growing antagonism to the line of Ögödei.
The opposition was led by another woman, the Nestorian
princess Sorghaqtani, widow of Tolui and mother of Möngke,
Hülegü, Kublai and Ariq-büke. Sorghaqtani, supported by
the powerful Batu, put forward the candidature of her eldest
son Möngke. Now, Eljigidei's loyalties were with the house
of Güyüg and he was well aware that his own position was
precarious. Unwilling, therefore, to commit himself, he did
not detain the mission, but sent Andrew and his companions
directly to Oghul Qaimish, whose camp was at the time in
the former dominion of Güyüg in the Emil-Tarbagatai
region.

The Western envoys' itinerary across Central Asia is not

known, except for a brief halt they made in Talas (modern Dzhambul in Kazakhstan), where Andrew noticed a group of German slaves belonging to Chaghatai's grandson Büri. At the regent's camp, which they reached at the beginning of 1250, more unpleasant experiences were in store for the Dominicans. Oghul Qaimish acknowledged the mission as if it were actually bringing the formal submission of the Christian West. Apparently she acted in this way to strengthen her position at court. As in Asia Frank was synonymous with European, the visit of envoys carrying gifts from the king of the Franks could easily be represented as an act of homage of the Western powers to Mongol sovereignty. Consequently she replied to Louis with a letter containing the usual Mongol formula for vassal lords, enjoining him to come and bring in person a yearly tribute in gold and silver, and threatening him with punishment if he did not obey. Accordingly there was, of course, no reference to Christianity or any alliance with the Franks. Her message was carried by Mongol envoys whom she despatched together with Andrew and his companions.

Meanwhile King Louis had landed in Egypt and after an initial success had met with a terrible reverse while attempting to march on Cairo. For the second time the Crusaders lost Damietta, and the king, captured by the Turks with his entire army, had to pay a heavy ransom for his release (6 May 1250). He spent the next four years in Palestine, mainly at Acre and Caesarea, trying to bring some order to the remnant of the Kingdom of Jerusalem.

It was at Caesarea, a small town just south of Haifa, that in April 1251 Andrew of Longjumeau came to report to the king. The account of the regent's reception and the tone of her letter shocked Louis who, according to his biographer Joinville (1224–1319), deeply regretted having sent the embassy. He would have been, perhaps, less disappointed had he realized that even in Eljigidei's letter a clear distinction had been made between the king of France, called 'magnificent king', and the Great Khan Güyüg who is referred to as 'king of the earth', i.e. universal monarch—a distinction which clearly implied a subservience of the former to the latter.

Andrew's mission, in spite of its obvious failure, is remarkable on more than one count. It was the second Western diplomatic mission to reach the heart of Asia, and the largest. Politically, it was the first and positive response of the West to the idea of a Mongol-Christian *entente*, for which the initiative came, it should not be forgotten, from the Mongols themselves. For this reason alone it must be regarded as having opened a new era in Mongol-European relations. It led, moreover, to the mission of William of Rubruck which is in itself one of the most remarkable events in the history of Europe's discovery of Asia.

VI

Friar William, the Missionary

IN SEARCH OF GERMAN SLAVES

A good deal has been written about Friar William's journey to Mongolia (1253–55) since the beginning of the nineteenth century. A frequent mistake is to represent it as yet another effort of King Louis of France to renew negotiations with the Mongol court after the failure of Andrew of Longjumeau's mission in 1250. In effect, William's mission was primarily religious in scope and it was undertaken on the initiative of the Flemish Franciscan himself.

Friar William was born at Rubruck, near Cassel in French Flanders, between 1215 and 1220. Hardly anything is known of his early life. He lived for some time in Paris, probably studying in a friary, and he was personally acquainted with King Louis. In 1248 he accompanied the king on his Crusade to Egypt and stayed with him in Palestine until 1252. There he met Andrew of Longjumeau from whom he learned about his journey to the Mongols and the condition of the Christians living under their rule. Andrew described to him the sad fate of Büri's German captives in Central Asia, cut off from the Church and without any spiritual comfort. From Andrew, William heard also about the Mongols' tolerant attitude towards foreign religions and the role and influence of the 'pernicious' Nestorian clerics in their society. This information corroborated what he already knew on the subject from the account of John of Pian di Carpine.

Friar William, a young and passionate man, was filled with the desire to convert the Mongols to true Christianity and bring consolation and help to the Christians living under their yoke. In this resolve he was also encouraged by reports of conversions of Mongol princes to the Christian faith which were reaching the king of France from various quarters. In particular, the news of the conversion of Sartaq, son of Batu, had spread far and wide among the Eastern Christians. It should be remembered that the middle of the thirteenth century was a period of great evangelical fervour, caused principally by the Council of Lyons' emphatic affirmation of the need to undertake missionary work on a world-wide scale, and that reports like this had had a profound effect on the clergy.

Nevertheless, it is doubtful whether Louis showed much enthusiasm for William's plan so soon after the rebuttal he had received from the Mongol court. He instructed William to make clear to the Mongol chiefs the unofficial character of his mission, and gave him only one letter, addressed to Sartaq, requesting permission for the friar to preach the Gospel and give spiritual help to the Christians scattered in his domain.

On the other hand, Louis knew the value of a fact-finding mission. Before William left Acre for Constantinople he asked him to report on all he should see among the Tartars, hoping no doubt to get in this way a better understanding of their intentions towards the West and the Moslem world.

William's party comprised the Italian Minorite Bartholomew of Cremona, a French secretary by the name of Gosset whom King Louis entrusted with various presents for the khan, and a dragoman, or interpreter, whose identity is not clear, but who appears to have been a Syrian Latin called Omodeo. He turned out to be a poor acquisition from every point of view. The goal of the journey was Sartaq's camp on the lower Volga.

The travellers left Acre at the beginning of 1253. After a brief stay at Constantinople to get supplies as well as information from the local merchants, they embarked for Soldaia in Crimea, whence they were to proceed by land to their destination.

They crossed the 'Greater Sea', as the Black Sea was then called, and reached Soldaia on 21 May. They stopped there just long enough to purchase some horses and ox-carts, and on 1 June they were on the move again.

Three days later, travelling in a northwesterly direction, they met the first Tartars. From that moment William, like Friar John, felt as if he 'were stepping into some other world'. In William's account of the journey, known as the *Itinerary*, his impressions are vividly and carefully recorded. From what he writes it seems that the Mongols had their doubts about the purpose of his mission and found it difficult to accept his statement that he had not been sent by the king of the Franks. When, after his two months' crossing of the south Russian steppe, he finally reached Sartaq's camp, the latter also assumed that he was Louis's emissary, and without delay directed him to his father Batu, whose camp was a three days' journey farther east, beyond the Volga.

Batu, in turn, did not allow the Franciscans to stay in his domain, and ordered them to continue their journey to Mongolia in order to obtain permission to carry out their ministry from the emperor himself. Batu obviously regarded the friars' explanations as ambiguous and inadequate, and felt that they should be dealt with by the highest authority. The great *quriltai* of 1251 had elected Möngke (*d.* 1259), the son of Tolui, as Great Khan, and it was to him at Karakorum that the Franciscans were instructed to report.

The election of Möngke had marked the definitive transfer of power from the Ögödeids to the Toluids. It had been achieved largely through Batu's support, a fact which accounts for Möngke's recognition of his cousin as the virtual ruler of the Mongol empire west of the Balkash. The enthronement was, as usual, followed by a harsh persecution of the defeated clan and its supporters. The regent Oghul Qaimish was executed and her policies were repudiated by the new emperor. Her son was banished and those members of the Chaghataid clan that had supported her were quietly eliminated, among them the same Prince Büri whose German slaves had caused so much concern in the West.

Möngke, a very able leader in the Chingis Khan tradition, aimed at revitalizing the empire by means of territorial conquest and a stricter enforcement of the Mongol law. In reshaping his foreign policy he could not avoid taking into account the situation in Europe and, in particular, the role of the French king who was then considered by the Mongols as the leading political figure in the West. This is also one of the reasons why Batu was so anxious that Möngke in person should interview the friars.

THE JOURNEY TO MÖNGKE'S ORDO

The journey of the two Franciscans across Central Asia followed by and large the route taken earlier by John and Benedict. With them went the interpreter Omodeo and a Mongol officer to act as guide and escort. The clerk Gosset was left behind as hostage. The distance between Batu's camp on the Volga and Möngke's *ordo* near Karakorum was covered in three and a half months. In the course of the journey Friar William took great pains to collect geographical and ethnographical information. Although, as we shall see, he was not such a diplomat as John of Pian di Carpine, Friar William was beyond question a keener observer of his surroundings. His report is one of the most important contributions to the physical geography of Central Asia until the nineteenth century. He discovered, among other things, the true character of the Caspian Sea, and was the first writer to give the correct course of the Don and the Volga. He was the first to positively identify the Grand Cathay, i.e. China, with the country of the Seres of classical times, although Friar John may have already suspected it. It is also from him that we hear for the first time of Tibet, which had fallen increasingly under Mongol control from 1240 onwards. He carefully compared the information collected on the way with that found in the classical and medieval works with which he was acquainted. In the *Itinerary* he records, for instance, how he enquired about the monsters and fabulous people described by Isidore of Seville and Solinus, and how astonished he was to find no evidence of their existence.

His interest in people's customs and beliefs was of course directly related to his desire to effect conversions; nevertheless his accurate description of foreign faiths and practices makes his report a document of prime importance and in many ways unique, as neither Friar John nor Marco Polo paid sufficient attention in their works to the spiritual culture of the people they described. In the *Itinerary* we find particularly valuable information on the distribution of Christian communities in Central Asia and Mongolia and the spread of Nestorianism. William, oddly enough, did not recognize that Sartaq himself was a Nestorian Christian, but he noticed that one of his chief dignitaries belonged to this faith and that there were Christians at his encampment. He comments also about the Christianity, of Greek rite, of the peoples of the Caucasus and especially of the Alans, many of whom had entered into the Mongols' service.

Just before leaving for Möngke's *ordo*, the friar, to his great surprise, met a Coman who greeted him in Latin. He turned out to be one of the Comans baptized and instructed by the Minorites in Hungary. Meetings like this must have raised William's hopes for the success of his mission. He was, as we know, anxious to find out more about the Christian captives held by the Mongols, and in particular about Büri's German slaves, whose plight had prompted him to undertake his mission in the first place. At both Sartaq's and Batu's camps William made enquiries about them, but all he could learn was that Büri had been recently put to death. To his distress he later found out that the whole German colony had been deported from Talas to the mining town of Bulad, in the Borotala valley in Dzungaria, where they were put to work in the mines and at smelting iron and forging weapons.

Sometime in October William and his party crossed the Chu and Ili rivers. In the valley of the Ili, south of Lake Balkash, William noticed that most of the towns had been destroyed 'so that the Tartars could feed their flocks there, for it is very fine pasturage'. This is one of several instances recorded in our sources of the Mongol traditional policy of converting ploughed land into pastures for their cattle and horses.

Riding westwards the travellers reached Cailac, or Qayaligh (near modern Kopal in east Kazakhstan), where they spent almost two weeks. Qayaligh was a big market town inhabited mostly by Moslem Turks. There were also Buddhist and Nestorian temples which William and Bartholomew had ample opportunity to investigate. William's description of Buddhist ritual, including the use of the famous formula *Om mani padme hum,* is the first of its kind in Western literature. Speaking of the Nestorians our friar mentions their use of the Sogdian language both in writing and in their liturgy. Now, throughout Asia the liturgical language of the Nestorian Church was Syriac. Sogdian, an Iranian language, had been once the *lingua franca* of Central Asia, but in the latter part of the first millennium it had progressively declined in favour of Eastern Turkish. William's remark is of great interest, as it shows that Sogdian was still in use in the middle of the thirteenth century. The Sogdian script was adopted by the Uighurs who, in turn, passed it to the Mongols. This fact too is mentioned by William who likewise noted the influence wielded by the Uighur scribes among the Tartars.

On 30 November the party left Qayaligh and resumed its journey across the Emil-Tarbagatai region, Dzungaria and the Altai, travelling now at great speed. For William who was, like Friar John, a heavy man, this fast ride across Central Asia was nothing short of an ordeal. He and his companions had a solid meal only once a day, in the evening, and this often consisted of almost raw mutton because of lack of fuel. Their Mongol guide was an arrogant and unpleasant man who enjoyed frightening his charges with hair-raising descriptions of the dangers lying ahead. He became, however, more human as the journey progressed, and in the end he even took the friars to the camps of Mongol chiefs so that they could recite prayers for them. It was on these occasions that William, as a missionary, experienced perhaps his greatest disappointment for, as he writes, 'if I had had a good interpreter this would have given me an opportunity of sowing much good seed.' Omodeo had, unfortunately, proved hopelessly unreliable, and our friars had eventually to give up any attempt at preaching.

William mentions here an interesting fact. The Mongol

chiefs whom the friars visited on their journey asked them about the pope and whether he was a man of great age, 'for they had heard that he was five hundred years old'. This question must have surprised our Franciscans. They were, of course, acquainted by now with the Mongols' peculiar practice of employing clerics of all faiths to pray for their prosperity, but they did not know that the Mongols, by associating worship and prayer with good fortune and long life (an idea borrowed from China), believed also that religious leaders could attain extreme longevity. The following episode from the life of Chingis Khan illustrates this point.

When Chingis was campaigning in Central Asia in 1219 he summoned to his camp the Chinese Taoist sage Ch'ang-ch'un, who claimed to be three hundred years old. He was actually only seventy. The conqueror questioned him about the technique to achieve immortality, to which the Taoist Patriarch replied that life can only be prolonged through sobriety, meditation and prayer. Chingis liked the elderly man and before sending him back he conferred important privileges on him, virtually making him the head of all Taoist and Buddhist temples in north China. He imposed as a condition, however, that the monks of these temples should hold religious services and pray regularly to Heaven for the emperor's health and good fortune. Ch'ang-ch'un remained on friendly terms with the conqueror until his death, a few days before that of Chingis, in 1227.

INTERVIEW WITH THE GREAT KHAN AND LIFE IN KARAKORUM

On 27 December the friars reached Möngke's *ordo*, just west of Karakorum. After a few days spent settling down at the camp and explaining the purpose of their journey to the chief scribe Bolghai, William and Bartholomew were eventually admitted to the august presence of the Great Khan on 4 January 1254.

Möngke, 'a flat-nosed man of medium height, about forty-five years old', was sitting on a couch in his sumptuous gold-lined tent, wearing 'a speckled and shiny fur like sealskin'. Next to him sat his young and beautiful third wife Baya'ujin. The emperor offered the friars the customary Mongol beverages: rice wine, kumys (Friar William's 'comos') and mead. William, through the interpreter Omodeo, told Möngke that he and his companion had come to preach Christianity, and requested to be allowed to carry out their ministry or, at least, to stay at the imperial camp until the following spring as Bartholomew was in poor health. Unfortunately, the interview was marred from the beginning as Omodeo was in a state of intoxication and so, apparently, was the emperor. Möngke showed displeasure on learning that the friars had gone to Sartaq first instead of going directly to him; nevertheless he allowed them to stay for two months at the *ordo*. When the audience was over, he had the friars thoroughly questioned by his secretaries about the kingdom of France and its wealth, clearly with the aim of extracting as much information as possible from his guests.

Instead of two months William spent about six months in the emperor's entourage, first at the *ordo* near Karakorum, then, from the beginning of April, at the Mongol capital itself. The friars seem to have been accepted by their patrons as two more members of the already numerous Nestorian clergy, and as such they enjoyed considerable freedom of movement.

Shortly after their arrival the Franciscans met a woman from Metz in Lorraine, called Paquette, who had been taken prisoner by the Mongols in Hungary and who was married to a Russian carpenter. Through her they learned about another captive, the Parisian artist and engineer William Boucher, who was working at the emperor's palace in Kara-korum. Boucher, a skilled goldsmith, sculptor and architect, was held in high esteem by the Mongols who were always greatly impressed by technical skill. The French artist had built a wonderful contrivance in Möngke's palace, a detailed description of which is given by William in his *Itinerary*. It was a 'magic fountain' made of solid silver and in the shape of a tree surrounded by lions which poured forth, with musical accompaniment, the favourite drinks of the emperor. Boucher had also decorated the Nestorian church at Kara-korum with beautiful images and carvings.

For our friars Boucher was a godsend. Not only were they able to get from him firsthand information on the Mongols, but the Frenchman's adopted son, who was fluent in Mongo-lian, proved invaluable as interpreter.

Although William, a former resident of Paris, was not im-pressed with the Mongol capital which he compared un-favourably to the village of Saint Denis, he found at Kara-korum a truly international society quite unlike any other city at the time. The 'European colony' comprised French-men, Germans, Hungarians, Slavs and at least one English-man, called Basil. They intermingled with Alans, Georgians, Armenians, Persians, Turks and Chinese. All these people worked for the Mongols in various capacities: Europeans, Western Asians, Persians and Turks mostly as craftsmen, merchants and scribes; the Chinese as artisans, especially potters and builders. William was impressed by the skill of the Chinese and intrigued by their writing system and paper money, both unknown in the West.

There was a constant flow of tradesmen to Karakorum from all parts of Asia, and with them came also adventurers, conjurers and impostors eager to profit from the Mongols' superstition and ignorance. Some of them posed as priests, others as ambassadors of foreign countries. People of all nationalities were found among the clergy: Chinese in the twelve Buddhist and Taoist temples, and Central and Western Asians in the two mosques and in the Nestorian church, each trying to outdo the other in gaining the favours of the Mongol princes.

Under Möngke the Nestorians were in a privileged position. Two leading personalities at the court, the Great Khan's mother, Princess Sorghaqtani, and his favourite wife Oghul Tutmish, now both dead, had been devout believers, and Ariq-büke, one of Möngke's younger brothers, was also sympathetic towards the Christians. The chief secretary Bolghai was a Nestorian Kereit like his former colleague Chinqai who, incidentally, had perished in the purges following Möngke's election. As for Möngke himself, he does not seem to have favoured any religion in particular. He attended the Christian services and even showed interest in William's Latin Gospel, but he bestowed equal attention on all the other faiths. Fundamentally he remained a shamanist, for we know that his dependence on the soothsayers was very great. Like Chingis Khan, whom he tried to emulate, he would not take any decision without first consulting the omens in the traditional Mongol way, that is by burning the shoulder-blade of a sheep. According to Friar William's informers, Möngke had not returned to Hungary solely because of the contrary advice given by his soothsayers. This, however, may be an exaggeration. A whole section of William's *Itinerary*, and one of the most valuable in the whole report, is devoted to the soothsayers and their practices, scapulimancy in particular.

Möngke's own profession of faith is recorded by William in

the following terms: 'We Mongols believe that there is but one God, by Whom we live and by Whom we die, and towards Him we have an upright heart. . . . But just as God gave different fingers to the hand so has He given different ways to men.' The simile of the fingers is also ascribed to Möngke by an almost contemporary Chinese Buddhist source which, however, makes him add that Buddhism is like the palm of the hand!

During the several months spent at Möngke's *ordo* and at Karakorum the Franciscan friars often found themselves in the company of Nestorian clerics, taking part in their ceremonies and in the religious services for the imperial family. On Easter Sunday, 12 April 1254, William had the satisfaction of celebrating Mass and administering Communion to many Christians in the Nestorian church at Karakorum. But at heart the Catholic missionary resented being assimilated to the Nestorian clergy, whom he severely criticized both on account of their ignorance and of their morals. His bitter complaints about their corrupt practices, such as bigamy, simony, usury and drunkenness, fill page after page of the *Itinerary*. It is true that the Nestorian beliefs and practices noted by William show the influence of the Mongol milieu and also some contamination by Buddhism (apparently one of the monks accepted the doctrine of transmigration of souls in animals); however, most of his criticism is far too severe. Considering that Mongol Nestorianism had been cut off from its source in Mesopotamia for so long, it is remarkable how little it had departed from its fundamental teaching. William's complaints stem chiefly from the frustration he experienced in carrying out his ministry and in reforming what he mistakenly regarded as a debased form of Christianity. The sum total of his missionary achievements was the conversion, *in articulo mortis*, of a Nestorian priest to the Church of Rome, and the baptism of six children, three of whom were the sons of a German captive.

William's failure was largely due to his own uncompromising attitude, and his sincere but tactless criticism of the other doctrines. This attracted the enmity of the Moslems and the antagonism of the Nestorians who, very friendly at first, later came to regard him as a trouble-maker. Unfavourable rumours about him began circulating and the value of his teaching was questioned. Möngke too seems to have found him too zealous and overbearing. King Hethum I of Lesser Armenia (1226–69), who visited Karakorum shortly after these events, was told there how Friar William had tried to convert the Great Khan by threatening him with hellfire. To this Möngke is reported to have replied, not without wisdom: 'The nurse at first lets some drops of milk into the infant's mouth, so that by tasting its sweetness he may be enticed to suck; only then does she offer him her breast. In the same way you should persuade Us, who seem to be totally unacquainted with this doctrine, in a simple and rational manner. Instead you immediately threaten Us with eternal punishments.'

In all fairness we must add that, adhering strictly to Louis's injunction, William had always denied being his envoy. Such a declaration had automatically deprived him of the right enjoyed by all official envoys to speak freely to the emperor whenever they wished. As a cleric he could answer questions only when summoned, and had to keep silent until questioned again. This, of course, greatly limited the opportunities of expounding his doctrine to the Great Khan.

When, towards the end of May, the disillusioned friar made enquiries about the prospect of going back, Möngke made no attempt to retain him. However, before sending him off he asked William to join the Nestorians in a public debate with the Moslems and the Buddhists. Three judges, one for each faith, were appointed, and Möngke issued a proclamation forbidding abusive language among the contestants and threatening with death anyone who hindered the proceedings.

The historic and somewhat incongruous debate took place on 30 May. William, with Boucher's son as interpreter, spoke first and took issue with the Buddhists on the existence of God and His attributes. He used theological arguments which were well beyond the comprehension of his opponents. The Nestorians next wished to have a debate with the Moslems who prudently withdrew from the discussion. They then began arguing with an Uighur Buddhist to whom they expounded on the coming of Christ, the Judgement, and the Trinity. All the people present listened without a word of contradiction, 'yet'—writes William—'not one of them said "I believe, I wish to become a Christian." ' When the debate was over 'the Nestorians and the Saracens alike sang loudly while the *tuins* (i.e. the Buddhist priests) kept silence, and afterwards they all drank their fill.' This, perhaps, better than any other description, gives an idea of the cultural context in which the Western missionary had to carry out his apostolate. The debate in which Friar William participated was the first of several religious disputes that took place at the Mongol court in the following decade. The representatives of Tibetan Buddhism eventually emerged as the real victors, a fact that accounts largely for the favour accorded to Lamaism by Möngke's successors.

MÖNGKE'S LETTER TO KING LOUIS AND FRIAR
WILLIAM'S RETURN

Having given William permission to leave, Möngke expressed his intention of appointing a Mongol envoy to carry a message for King Louis. The friar emphatically objected to this plan on the grounds that the journey was full of dangers and that he could not vouch for the ambassador's safety in Europe. William feared, not unreasonably, that any accident involving the Mongol would have given Möngke a pretext for invading Europe. Möngke in the end agreed to provide an escort only as far as Armenia, and asked William to deliver his message to Louis.

The original document issued by Möngke is lost, but its content is summarized in a somewhat garbled fashion in the *Itinerary*. From internal evidence it appears to have consisted of two separate parts, a formal edict and the letter itself. The edict, identical in tenor to that delivered by Eljigidei to Ascelinus, reaffirmed the divine origin of the emperor's command and the recipient's duty to abide by it. In the letter Möngke repudiated the earlier diplomatic exchanges under Güyüg and Oghul Qaimish ('how could that wicked woman, more vile than a dog, know about matters of war and affairs of peace?'), and enjoined King Louis to send envoys to show his willingness to be at peace with the Mongols.

Although the emperor gives as his aim the unification of the world 'from sunrise to sunset' under Mongol rule, the letter contains, significantly, no mention of tribute. The Great Khan at the time (1254) was not seeking any collaboration with the Franks against the Moslems, but he knew that their help might be useful later in the war against the Islamic world which his younger brother Hülegü had just begun. Möngke felt it was sufficient to remind the West of his power and far-reaching arm, and this is apparently all his letter to Louis was meant to achieve.

Friar Bartholomew did not return with William. Fearing the return journey because of ill health, he obtained permission to stay in Karakorum under the friendly care of

Boucher. Presumably he ended his days there, the first missionary and, as far as we know, the first Italian to die in the Far East.

William and his escort left about 10 July. As they were now travelling in summer, they took the shorter route north of Lake Balkash. On 14 September they arrived at Batu's camp where they found their servants and the clerk Gosset. After spending a month with Batu they proceeded southwards following the Volga to its delta. On the way they visited the khan's newly built capital, Sarai, and were probably among the first European travellers to see this city, which recent excavations have partly brought to light. The party then entered the territory of the Alans and, crossing the Derbent Pass and the eastern Caucasus, reached the plain of Mughan south of the Kura river. After a brief stay at Baiju's camp the travellers proceeded to Turkey via Nakhichevan, where William celebrated Christmas. At Ani, between Yerevan and Kars, they met a group of five Dominican friars who were making their way to Central Asia. They had been sent by Innocent to carry out their ministry among Büri's German slaves, of whose existence the pope had also been informed. William told them about his own experiences and dissuaded them from proceeding further with their plan.

By way of Erzerum, Kayseri and Konya, the Minorite and his companions eventually reached the port of Lajazzo in the Gulf of Alexandretta. There they embarked for Cyprus. When the weary and much-travelled friar finally arrived in Nicosia he found, to his great disappointment, that he could not return to France and report to King Louis as promised. Instead he was sent by his Provincial back to Palestine where shortly after he was appointed lecturer in Theology at Acre. In the weeks following his arrival in the Holy Land William wrote his famous report which he sent, sometime in 1255, to the French monarch with a plea to be temporarily released from duty so that he could visit him in Paris.

We know, indirectly, that this request was granted. His illustrious contemporary, the English Franciscan philosopher Roger Bacon (*c.* 1220–92), was interested in the geographical material of the *Itinerary*, which he quotes at length in his encyclopaedic *Opus Majus*. Bacon mentions that he collated the text of the *Itinerary* with the help of its author; he must, therefore, have met William during his stay in Paris in the years 1257–67. This is the only reference to our Franciscan in contemporary sources. The date and place of his death are unknown.

William's work has survived in a number of manuscripts which derive from three codices, all found in England. After three centuries of oblivion, the *Itinerary* was discovered and published by Richard Hakluyt and Samuel Purchas. Only in recent times, however, have scholars in the West been able to appreciate fully the value of Friar William's report. Its rich store of information is still helping historians and archaeologists in their investigations. Whether it is the role of women in Mongol society or the activity of the Genoese and Venetian merchants in the Near East, there is hardly a topic on which William does not contribute some interesting remarks. His detailed description of Karakorum and its buildings has been an invaluable guide for the Soviet and Mongolian archaeologists during the excavations on the site of the old capital in 1948–49. The linguist can also benefit from William's transcription of foreign words (he had a much better ear than John of Pian di Carpine), and from his remarks on language affinities.

Compared with these contributions, the purely historical information on the Mongols found in the *Itinerary* is rather disappointing. William was no historian and the facts recorded in his work are garbled and unreliable. Much of his information derived from oral accounts of the Nestorians at Karakorum who, as William himself soon found out, were wont 'to make a great story out of nothing'. From them he obtained a new variant of the Prester John legend which is not without interest.

In this version King John is identified with the Naiman Küchlüg, while Ong-khan (William's 'Unc') appears as King John's brother and successor. Unc fought against Chingis Khan and, after having been defeated by the latter, fled to China. His daughter was captured by Chingis who gave her as wife to one of his sons, and it was from them that Möngke was born.

This story is based on several misunderstandings, the most curious of which is Unc's flight to China. We know from the *Secret History* that Ong-khan never went to China, but met his death in western Mongolia. Now, in the Ordos region in north China there lived the Christian Öngüt. As mentioned earlier, these Turkish tribes had sided with Chingis in 1204, and the conqueror had later rewarded their king by giving his daughter to him in marriage. From then on it had become customary for Mongol princesses to marry into the Öngüt royal family. William's account originates from a phonetic similarity between Unc and Öngüt—both, incidentally, deriving from the Chinese word meaning 'king'—and from a garbled report of the relationship by marriage between Chingis Khan, the Ong-khan, and the Öngüt ruler. This fact is worth noting because an identical confusion was also responsible for Marco Polo's later identification of Prester John with the Ong-khan. Marco, however, carried phonetic assimilation to extremes by identifying the Öngüt kingdom with the country of Gog and Magog, names which according to him correspond to Unc and Mongol!

Friar William ends his report to the king of France with some practical advice. In his view, friars should not be sent to the Tartars without proper credentials. The best course would be for the pope to appoint a bishop and send him as an official envoy, so as to ensure that he would be listened to; besides, he would need a good interpreter, 'nay, several interpreters, and abundant supplies'. At the same time, William urges the Church and Christian Europe to unite and conquer the lands in Asia Minor that had been invaded by the Mongols: 'I say to you with confidence, if your peasants, I will not say kings and knights, were willing to go as do the kings of the Tartars and be content with the same kind of food, they could take possession of the whole world.'

Beyond doubt the mission of the Flemish Franciscan had also failed in its aim to convert the Tartars and in any other political objectives it may have had. Möngke's arrogant letter could not but further disappoint and hurt King Louis, and dispel any hopes he might have retained of a Christian-Mongol *entente*. William's report, moreover, contributed to shattering the West's lingering dream about Prester John's or King David's co-operation in the crusading movement.

VII

The Mongol Crusade

THE MONGOLS AND THE NEAR EAST

Frederick II died in 1250, but the struggle between the papacy and the Hohenstaufen continued to tear Italy apart for] two more decades. The emperor's son and successor, Conrad IV, was a mediocre personality, possessing none of his father's gifts and enjoying little of his prestige. He died [in 1254 leaving the throne of Sicily and Jerusalem to his two-year-old son Conradin. But Conradin was displaced by Frederick's natural son Manfred who soon resumed hostilities with the Church. By this time, however, the pope had secured the support of a strong ally in the person of Charles of Anjou, the proud brother of King Louis of France. Pope Clement IV invested Charles as King of Sicily in 1265 and in the following year the Angevin defeated Manfred who was killed in battle. Conradin's attempt to restore the family fortunes also ended in disaster. His army was routed near Tagliacozzo and the young king, who had been taken prisoner, was executed in Naples on 29 October 1268. Conradin was the last of the Hohenstaufen.

The feud between Frederick and the Church had ended in the destruction of his house and the unfortunate alliance of the papacy and the Angevins which was to be a major factor in shaping the history of Europe for the rest of the century.

While the death of Frederick brought about a number of fundamental changes in the structure of power in Europe, an important, but quite independent, redistribution of power took place at the same time in the Near East. Here two events were mainly responsible: the Mongol push into Western Asia and Mesopotamia and the rise of the Mameluk Turks in Egypt. The immediate effect of the ensuing Egyptian-Mongol confrontation was a new attempt on the part of the Mongols to seek that alliance with the European nations which the earlier diplomatic exchanges had failed to achieve.

Shortly after Möngke's election Hülegü, a younger brother of the Great Khan Möngke, had been put in charge of the expedition against the Moslem East. Hülegü was eager to carry out this task successfully because it had been agreed that his territorial conquests would form the patrimony of his branch of the imperial family.

In Persia the Mongols controlled Khorassan and a number of districts which were under the administration of military chiefs often at odds with each other. Much of the country was ruled by semi-independent local dynasties which posed no serious threat to Hülegü's work of reunification.

The major challenge to the Mongols came from the Assassins. These dedicated members of the heterodox Ismaili sect of Islam founded at the end of the eleventh century, and notorious in the West for its terrorist practices, had a powerful hold in eastern Persia. Hülegü's brilliant campaign of 1256–57, which ended with the capture of the reputedly impregnable fortress of Alamut in the Elburz Mountains and the surrender of the Ismaili leader, virtually wiped out the Persian branch of the sect.

This feat was immediately acclaimed by all the Sunnite Moslems, who saw in Hülegü a defender of orthodox Islam.

But their joy was short-lived. Hülegü's next objective was, in fact, the Abbasid Caliphate whose leader was regarded as the spiritual head of Islam. Baghdad was invested by the Mongols and fell, after a fierce siege, in February 1258. The magnificent city of Harun al-Rashid and the *Arabian Nights* was mercilessly plundered and burnt, and most of its population massacred. The Caliph was seized and slain. According to a popular but not reliable account, Hülegü caused him to die of hunger surrounded by his treasure to punish him for his avarice.

It would be a grave mistake, however, to think that Hülegü's campaign was prompted by religious considerations. By removing the Grand Master of the Ismaili sect and the Caliph of Baghdad, the two leading figures in the Moslem world, the Mongol prince hoped to weaken the political power of Islam and bring to a speedy end the conquest of Syria and Egypt.

Hülegü was well aware that the war against the Moslem sultanates could not fail to draw the sympathy and support of the Eastern Christians to him. The news of the fall of Baghdad was received by them with unrestrained jubilation, for it was regarded as a just retribution for over five centuries of Islamic oppression. Hülegü already had the military support of King Hethum of Armenia who, in 1254, had promised to supply the Mongol army with auxiliary troops. Möngke in return had promised him to respect the Christian communities in Asia Minor and, on completion of the war, return the Holy Places to the Christians. Hethum's son-in-law, Bohemond VI of Antioch, had also joined the 'Mongol Crusade'. It was a well-known fact that Hülegü's influential wife Doquz Khatun, a niece of the Ong-khan of the Kereits, was a devout Nestorian. Many members of Hülegü's entourage were also Christian, including his leading general Kitbuqa.

In January 1260 the Mongols conquered Aleppo and a month later Kitbuqa entered Damascus. The road to Jerusalem lay open ahead. It looked then as if the whole Moslem world would soon be engulfed by a Christian-Mongol tidal wave in a belated fulfilment of the Prester John prophecies! But the Mongols and their Christian allies had not reckoned with the Mameluks.

These Turkish slave troops of the Ayyubid sultans had come to power in Egypt in 1250, in fact during King Louis's captivity, by deposing their masters and electing a leader from their own ranks. In the following years the usurpers had consolidated their rule and made preparations to meet the Mongol threat. It is doubtful, however, whether they would have been able to withstand such a formidable enemy had it not been for the sudden death of Möngke in 1259. The emperor had been campaigning in western China when he fell victim to an epidemic of dysentery and died, aged only fifty.

As soon as Hülegü received the news he issued a peremptory order of submission to Egypt and returned to Persia, leaving Kitbuqa in charge of the operations. The Mongol army in Syria, now substantially reduced in size, had to contend also with the hostility of the Frankish barons who viewed the Mongol advance with increasing concern. When the Mameluk and the Mongol armies finally met at Ain Jalut in Galilee on 23 September 1260 the Mongols suffered a crushing defeat. General Kitbuqa was captured and was soon after executed by the victorious sultan Qutuz.

Just as twenty years earlier Christendom and Europe had been saved by the providential demise of Ögödei, so Moslem civilization survived what could have been a fatal blow thanks to the equally providential death of Möngke. The battle of Ain Jalut was another turning-point in history, for it not only checked the Mongol expansion towards the Mediterranean, but it also ensured Egyptian supremacy in the Near East for two and a half centuries, i.e. until the Ottoman conquest (1517). Furthermore, as it turned out, the fate of both the Frankish possessions of *Outremer* and the native Christians in the Near East were also sealed at Ain Jalut.

The immediate outcome of the battle was the recapture of Aleppo and Damascus by the Turks and the momentous rise of Baibars (1260–77), an ambitious Mameluk officer who had distinguished himself in fighting the Mongols.

Shortly after Kitbuqa's defeat Baibars led a coup against his master Qutuz, slew him and had himself elected sultan. He was the real founder of the Mameluk empire and one of the most interesting and colourful personalities in Moslem history. Shrewd, ruthless and brave in battle, his life-story reads like a novel. He was a legend already in his own time, and after his death his exploits became a favourite theme in popular romances.

Once in control of Egypt, Baibars's chief concern was to extend his rule over both Syria and Palestine while keeping the Mongols at bay. In successive campaigns and through subtle diplomatic work he gained control of the Ayyubid dominions in Syria, and in less than ten years he dislodged the Franks from some of their most cherished possessions, such as Caesarea, Antioch and the Krak des Chevaliers (1265–71).

To frustrate the Mongols' attempt to reconquer Syria, Baibars concluded an alliance with Batu's brother Berke, who had become khan of the Golden Horde in 1258. Berke had been converted to Islam—the first Mongol ruler to embrace this faith—and was opposed to Hülegü's campaign against the Moslems. Moreover, he resented Hülegü's occupation of the rich and commercially important Azerbaijan territory which he regarded as part of Batu's dominion.

After the destruction of the Caliphate, Berke's opposition to his cousin turned into open hostility. His contingent in Hülegü's army was ordered to defect to the Mameluks, an action which was partly responsible for Kitbuqa's defeat. Soon after Berke exchanged embassies with Baibars and declared war on Hülegü, thus effectively preventing him from carrying out an all-out offensive against the Mameluks.

Hülegü did achieve, however, the internal reunification of Persia. He ruled over this country as the first Ilkhan or Viceroy until his death in 1265. The title of Ilkhan (lit. 'subject khan') borne by his successors indicated the subservience of the Hülegids to the Great Khan of the Mongol empire.

After the death of Möngke in China, the supreme dignity had been assumed by his younger brother Qubilai, better known in the West as Kublai Khan. Kublai, who had also been campaigning in China, was elected emperor there by his army in a hasty and unconstitutional way. Simultaneously another brother of Möngke, Ariq-büke, was elected at Karakorum by his own followers.

In the subsequent conflict between the two rival brothers Hülegü sided with Kublai, whom he acknowledged as the legitimate sovereign. Ariq-büke was eventually defeated in 1264. Hülegü's early support for Kublai established a close bond between the Ilkhans of Persia and the Mongol emperor now residing in China, and until the end of the century the Ilkhans were regularly invested with their authority by the court in Khanbaliq (Peking).

DIPLOMATIC CONTACTS WITH THE ILKHANS

Hülegü was less successful in his efforts to win over the Western powers. True, his friendly attitude towards the Christians in Persia and in Syria was known at the papal court through reports coming from Byzantium and from the mendicant friars in the Levant. Among the Nestorians and the other Eastern Christians Hülegü and his wife were openly hailed as a new Constantine and Helena. It is also true, however, that both the Church and the Western nations were still ill informed about internal Mongol affairs and found it difficult to reconcile these encouraging reports from the Near East with the obvious hostility of the Mongols of Russia, whose renewed incursions into Poland seemed to confirm the persistent rumours about a forthcoming invasion of Europe. Relying on past experience, the Church had every reason to mistrust and fear the Mongols. This explains why, following Hülegü's invasion of Syria in 1257, Pope Alexander IV had urged the Latins to oppose the Mongols and had condemned those Christian leaders who, like Prince Bohemond of Antioch, had lent support to the invading army. In 1260 some Crusaders had actually left for the Holy Land to defend it against the Tartars. At the same time an effort was made to probe the Mongols' intentions by sending an embassy to Hülegü led by the English Dominican David of Ashby. The Christian envoys were welcomed by the Ilkhan who not only gave assurances that the Frankish possessions would be protected, but also promised that the Latin missionaries in Mongol-occupied territory would be exempted from taxes.

Although Hülegü's goodwill failed to alter the Franks' resolution to withstand the Mongol invasion, the reverse suffered by Kitbuqa and the momentous rise of Baibars caused some re-thinking in the Western camp. In some quarters it was felt that Baibars represented a more serious threat to Christianity in the Holy Land than the Tartars, and that the destruction of Mameluk power was a concrete issue on which the interests of Europe and those of the Ilkhan coincided.

This time Hülegü took the initiative. A Mongol mission comprising several people was sent by him to the pope and the kings of Europe in 1263–64 with proposals for a joint action against the Moslems. The battle of Ain Jalut had irretrievably shattered the myth of a Mongol superiority based on divine support, and the Mongol leaders were now compelled to deal with the Western rulers as equals. The embassy was, however, intercepted in Sicily by Manfred and forced to re-embark. Only one of its members managed to reach Rome and convey Hülegü's message to Pope Urban IV (1261–64).

Urban's reply was cautious, yet friendly. The pontiff praised the Mongol prince for his humane treatment of the Christians and urged him to accept baptism as other members of his family were reported to have done already.

By the time the papal message reached Persia, Hülegü had died. His son Abagha, who succeeded him as Ilkhan (1265–1282), was a Buddhist, but he had a high regard for Christianity as his mother, Doquz Khatun, and his wife Maria, daughter of the Emperor Michael VIII Palaeologus of Byzantium, were both Christian.

The new Ilkhan was anxious to pursue his father's policy and conclude an alliance with the West. Caught between the Golden Horde and the Mameluks, and threatened also by his Chaghataid cousins in Turkestan, he found himself in an unenviable situation. Aleppo and Damascus were in Baibars's hands, the army of the Mongols' staunchest ally, King Hethum, had been defeated, and Lesser Armenia had been overrun and ravaged by the Egyptians (1266).

Shortly after his accession Abagha sent a diplomatic mission to Pope Clement IV (1265–68), and from then on the exchange of embassies between the Ilkhanid capital Tabriz and the courts of Europe was continuous.

151

The situation had, indeed, reversed. Whereas before the West had vainly sought the friendship of the proud Tartars, now they in turn did not spare any efforts to woo the Western powers. Knowing that the pope regarded the Ilkhans' acceptance of baptism as a prerequisite for any political alliance, the Mongol ambassadors did not hesitate to spread the news of their master's imminent conversion to the Church of Rome. Even Hülegü, it was claimed, had considered becoming a Catholic just before his death. Similar rumours had been circulated before and were met now with incredulity and suspicion. Moreover, the idea of a military alliance with the Tartars was still repugnant to many a Christian leader. The diversion of the Eighth Crusade to Tunis showed clearly the unwillingness of the participants to become partners of the Mongols who, it was argued, after the defeat of the Mameluks would undoubtedly turn against their allies.

Only England seems to have realized the advantages of an alliance with the Ilkhans. After the death of King Louis near Tunis in 1270 and the end of his Crusade, Prince Edward, the son and heir of Henry III, planned a Crusade of his own against the Mameluks. On his arrival at Acre in the spring of the following year he sent an embassy to Abagha to coordinate a joint plan of attack. At the time, however, the Ilkhan's main army was deployed in Turkestan and only a small contingent, about ten thousand men, was sent to Syria. The Mongols, successful at first, were in the end forced back by Baibars's larger army. Edward's attempt, truly remarkable from the strategic point of view, failed also for lack of troops, and the prince sailed back to England in 1272.

Undaunted by the failure of this first concerted campaign Abagha continued his efforts to organize a Mongol-Western Crusade. The Dominican friar David of Ashby, who had stayed on in Persia, was sent back to Europe in 1273 to accompany a Mongol mission to the XIV Ecumenical Council, which was convoked by the new pope, Gregory X (1272–76), at Lyons in 1274.

Before his election Gregory had been at Acre with Edward and had gained a first-hand knowledge of the situation in the Near East. He was genuinely interested in a new Crusade, and in the possibility of a Christian-Tartar alliance. The main items on the agenda of the Council were the reform of the Church, the union with the Greek Church and the liberation of the Holy Land. Shortly after its opening, the sixteen-man mission from Abagha arrived in Lyons. David of Ashby, who had spent almost fifteen years among the Mongols, acted as interpreter. He also prepared, for the benefit of the assembly, a report 'On the Deeds of the Tartars', the only known manuscript of which was unfortunately lost in a fire in Turin in 1904. Abagha's letter was read at the Council, which was favourably impressed by his protestation of friendship and by his offer to co-operate in spreading Christianity and fighting the Moslems. To create an even more favourable climate, three members of the Mongol delegation asked to be baptized. The ceremony was conducted by the Bishop of Ostia, the future Pope Innocent V, but it is doubtful whether this dramatic act on the part of Abagha's envoys convinced all those present for, as one chronicler later put it, 'God knows well for what purpose they did it.'

The Council ended its works passing a resolution in favour of a new Crusade. The Mongol ambassadors left with the promise that the crusading army would send envoys to Abagha to plan a joint strategy before its arrival in the Holy Land. We know, indirectly, that Gregory was aware that Abagha's offer was prompted mainly by his desire to reconquer Syria. He was, nevertheless, so eager to promote the

Crusade that he was prepared to accept the Ilkhan's partnership without even insisting, as his predecessors had done, on the Mongol ruler's formal acceptance of baptism.

Abagha promptly reacted by sending two envoys to the pope in 1276. This was followed a year later by an embassy to Europe which reached as far as London. However, the death of Gregory in 1277 suspended indefinitely the realization of his project. In England Edward was too busy with the war in Wales to become involved in a Crusade which lacked both the support of the European nations and the co-operation of the Frankish barons of *Outremer*. Thus, when Baibars died, also in 1277, neither the West nor the Mongols took advantage of the political confusion in Egypt following the death of the sultan. When his successor Qalawun was elected two years later, Mameluk power was still intact.

THE CHURCH RESUMES HER MISSIONS TO THE TARTARS

Although the dialogue between the Mongol court and Europe continued for the next three decades, largely through the initiative of the Ilkhans for whom the Moslem Turks were an all too visible reality, the West was no longer interested in military ventures to liberate the Holy Sepulchre. The crusading spirit had died with St. Louis. Gregory's attempt to revive it was probably doomed in advance because of the magnitude of the task and the shortsightedness of the Franks who, until the very end, preferred to negotiate with Egypt rather than join forces with the Mongols. Much of the blame for their attitude falls upon Charles of Anjou (*d*. 1285) whose opposition to the Tartars stemmed from the friendly relations that they entertained with Byzantium, which Charles wished to incorporate in his Mediterranean empire.

The situation was further complicated by the rivalries of the Italian maritime republics. Commercial interests played, as is well known, a paramount role in the later Crusades. Both Genoa and Venice carried on an extremely profitable trade with Egypt and Syria. After the fall of the Latin Empire in 1261 Genoa, through its alliance with Michael Palaeologus, had replaced Venice in Byzantium and in the Black Sea ports, gaining control of the Central Asian trade and becoming, in this way, a natural partner of the Mongols of Persia. As a result Venice turned to the Golden Horde, and in her foreign policy supported those factions in *Outremer* that were in favour of an alliance with the Mameluks against the Ilkhans.

Thus, in the latter part of the century disunion among the European powers involved in the Near East was almost complete, nor did any personality emerge strong enough to reconcile such disparate and conflicting political, religious and economic interests. The outcome, predictably enough, was the final loss in a matter of a few years of the last Frankish possession in *Outremer* when Acre fell to the Mameluks on 18 May 1291.

After the death of Gregory X political developments in Italy, culminating with the Sicilian Vespers (1282), had forced the Church to concentrate her efforts and resources in restoring the power of the Angevins. Unable and unwilling to sponsor a military action in the Levant, the popes of this period reverted in their relations with the Mongols to a policy of religious propaganda.

Since the early mission of John of Pian di Carpine and throughout the subsequent diplomatic exchanges, the conversion of the Mongols had been one of the principal aims of the Church, as evident from all the bulls issued by the papal chancellery.

The journey from China to Italy of the Venetian merchants Niccolò and Maffeo Polo in 1269 had revived interest in Rome for a Christian mission to be sent to the heart of the Mongol empire. Kublai had asked the pope through the Polos to send him a hundred masters of the liberal arts and some oil from the lamp burning at the Holy Sepulchre in Jerusalem. Pope Gregory had responded to the Great Khan's request by appointing two learned Dominican friars as his legates to the Mongol court. Regrettably the two Dominicans lost heart on the way and turned back without fulfilling their mission, while the Polo brothers and Niccolò's seventeen-year-old son Marco continued their exciting journey to Cathay. Their travels and adventures in Central Asia and China, where they resided for about sixteen years (1275–91), are well known through Marco's vivid description and we shall not dwell upon them here.

The missionary movement took a more active turn in 1278 with the establishment by Pope Nicholas III of Franciscan friaries in Gazaria (Crimea). From there the Minorites extended their activity to Sarai and began preaching to the Mongols of the Golden Horde, the Comans and the other people of the Kipchak steppe. The two Franciscan Custodies of Gazaria and Sarai flourished at the end of the thirteenth and the beginning of the fourteenth century largely through the support of the Genoese merchants whose commercial interests, centred on the lucrative slave trade, extended practically over the whole Golden Horde dominion. Among the Franciscans' successes was the conversion of several members of the Mongol ruling family including, apparently, even Batu's great-grandson Toqtai Khan (1291–1312). However, Toqtai's successor, the famous khan Özbeg (1313–41), was a Moslem convert and under him Islam became finally the official religion of the court. Before long the Moslem faith spread among the Mongols and the Comans, making the work of the Catholic missionaries of 'Northern Tartary' (Tartaria Aquilonaris) increasingly difficult and hazardous. One of the signal contributions of the Franciscans of south Russia is the so-called *Codex Cumanicus*, a Latin-Coman-Persian dictionary compiled in the Crimea about 1295, which is our main source on the Coman language.

Again in the year 1278, Pope Nicholas sent a five-man Franciscan mission to Tabriz with instructions to proceed to the court of Kublai. They were to expound the Christian teaching to the Great Khan who was reported to have embraced Christianity. The friars reached Persia, but for unknown reasons never went as far as China.

The next, and by far the most important, mission to the Tartars was that of the Italian Minorite John of Montecorvino (1247–1328). His journey to China was prompted in large measure by the historic visit to Europe of the Nestorian prelate Rabban Sauma, to which we must now briefly refer.

THE MISSION OF RABBAN SAUMA TO EUROPE

Bar Sauma ('Son of Fasting'), better known as Rabban Sauma, was a Turk probably of Öngüt origin, born in Peking about 1225. He became a monk, and with a disciple called Mark, who was also a Nestorian Öngüt, left China to go on a pilgrimage to Jerusalem. The two crossed Central Asia following the regular route from Tangut (Ninghsia) to Persia which the Polos also used when they went to China.

Prevented by the political situation from reaching the Near East, Sauma and Mark spent several years in Persia. In 1281 Mark was unexpectedly elected Patriarch of the Nestorians, under the name of Mar Yahballaha III. Sauma was soon after appointed Visitor General. When, a few years later, the Ilkhan Arghun (1284–91) looked for a suitable envoy to send to Europe to conclude the long-sought alliance with the Christian nations, Mar Yahballaha recommended his former teacher. Besides diplomatic skill, Sauma had also a knowledge of Persian, a language for which interpreters could always be found among the Italian merchants.

The Nestorian cleric sailed from Constantinople to Naples and reached Rome in the summer of 1287. There he was received by the cardinals, as Pope Honorius IV had died only a few months earlier and the new pope had not yet been elected.

In Rome, Sauma, although treated as a guest of honour, was closely questioned on theological problems. He impressed the Curia with his straightforwardness and modesty. His final remark after a harrowing session with the inquisitive cardinals is justly famous: 'I have come from distant lands not to discuss or to teach my beliefs, but to pay my respects to my lord the Pope and to the relics of the Saints, and to deliver the messages of the king and of the Catholicos. If you please let us have done with discussions. If you will order someone to show me the churches and the tombs of the Saints which are here you will do your servant and disciple a great kindness.'

Sauma then proceeded to Paris where he was the guest of Philip IV the Fair (1268–1314), and thence to Bordeaux to meet King Edward I. He delivered to these monarchs the letter of Arghun and was everywhere treated with great respect. Philip even promised to send an army to help Arghun when the Ilkhan decided to start his offensive against Egypt.

On learning that Nicholas IV had been elected pope, Sauma returned to Rome in the spring of the following year.

For several more weeks he enjoyed the lavish hospitality of the papal court. As he called himself an Eastern Christian (Nestorians never referred to themselves as Nestorians) and professed allegiance to the pope and the Church of Rome, Sauma was accepted as a Catholic and was allowed to take part in religious ceremonies at St. Peter's. He left bearing rich gifts, holy relics, and letters to Arghun and Mar Yah-ballaha. The pope urged the Ilkhan to accept baptism and the Patriarch to instruct the faithful in the teachings of the Roman Church.

On his return to Persia Sauma wrote an account of his memorable experiences in Europe which is of immense historical and antiquarian interest, as it represents the contemporary Eastern counterpart of Marco Polo's description of Asia.

The Nestorian's visit to Rome and the description that he gave of the Mongol empire emphasized the need, already felt within the Church, to spread Christianity in farther Asia. Nicholas IV (1288–92) had been himself a General of the Franciscan Order and was eager to promote evangelical work. The arrival of John of Montecorvino in Italy two years later made the first mission to China possible.

VIII

The Archbishop of Khanbaliq

JOHN OF MONTECORVINO'S JOURNEY TO CHINA

Friar John was born in Montecorvino, now in Salerno province, Italy, in 1247. He spent several years as a Franciscan missionary in Armenia and Persia before returning to Italy in 1289 as legate of King Hethum II. The Armenian monarch, son of Hethum I, wanted to inform the pope of the situation in his country and request assistance from the West to ward off the Moslem danger which had then become particularly acute.

John conveyed the royal message to Nicholas in Rieti, reporting to him at the same time on the state of Christianity in the East. He probably confirmed the current reports about Kublai's friendly attitude to Christianity. The earlier mission of the Polo brothers, the letters of Arghun and the recent journey of Rabban Sauma had all indicated that the Great Khan protected the Christians of his realm and was interested in their faith. To this we must add that when these events took place, in the latter part of the thirteenth century, there was already in Europe a good deal of interest in the Kingdom of Cathay. This had been aroused by the Italian traders who for some time had been importing cheap silk, the so-called 'Cathay Silk', from China via the Crimea and Tana (present-day Azov) in the Don delta, as well as through Baghdad. Since the mendicant friars in south Russia and the Near East worked in close association with the Latin traders, there was a constant trickle of information on Central and Eastern Asia reaching Europe.

Encouraged by all these reports, Nicholas IV decided to repeat the attempt of Nicholas III and send a new Franciscan mission to Cathay. Five friars were again chosen, and John of Montecorvino was appointed as leader. Like their predecessors they too carried the pope's goodwill letters to monarchs and religious leaders of the Orient.

John and his companions sailed, almost certainly from Venice, to the port of Lajazzo and thence proceeded by land to Antioch, Sis and Tabriz. On the way they delivered the papal messages to the Patriarch of the Jacobites and King Hethum, and to the Ilkhan Arghun and the Nestorian Patriarch Mar Yahballaha.

John spent several months preaching in Tabriz where the Minorites had a convent and a church which they shared with the Dominican friars. When, sometime in 1291, he resumed his journey his five confrères, presumably detained in Persia by other duties, were no longer with him. Instead he had two new companions, the Dominican Nicholas of Pistoia, and an Italian merchant called Peter of Lucalongo who had business in China.

Rather than follow the usual caravan route across Central Asia which was unsafe at the time owing to a war between Kublai and his rebel cousin Qaidu, the travellers took the less common and much longer sea route.

They embarked at Hormuz, in the Persian Gulf, landing about a month later at Quilon on the west coast of India. From Quilon they gained, also by sea, the Coromandel coast and visited the Christian community at Mylapore near Madras. Nicholas of Pistoia died there and was buried by Montecorvino in the famous Church of St. Thomas.

According to a letter written several years later from China, John spent thirteen months in India travelling and carrying out missionary work. He claims to have baptized a hundred people in this period. A lengthy report which our friar apparently wrote when he was at Mylapore is the first description of south India by a European, as it precedes by seven years Marco Polo's account. In it John describes the exotic flora of the country, noting in particular its spices. He mentions also several local customs and practices, such as writing on palm leaves, cremation of the dead (but not *sati*) and Indian eating habits, on the whole showing, however, little real understanding of Indian culture. In his astronomical and climatic observations of the tropics, more accurate than those of the Venetian traveller, we have perhaps the first reference to the Southern Cross.

During his stay in India John of Montecorvino enquired about the Terrestrial Paradise and the fabulous beings traditionally associated with this country. Echoing William of Rubruck he also wrote 'none of these things could I find.'

John, and Peter of Lucalongo, left India in 1292, or early in 1293. The Polos, who had probably begun their return journey at the beginning of 1291, must have reached the Malabar coast—Malabar was the name then applied to the south Indian coast from Nellore to Quilon—before John's departure. However, there is no indication that the two groups of Italians met on Indian soil.

Of John's voyage from India to China through the Straits of Malacca we possess no information. Presumably he and his companion landed at Zaiton (Chüanchow) in Fukien. Thence they proceeded to the Mongol capital, Khanbaliq, where they arrived in 1294, shortly after the death of Kublai Khan.

The great Mongol emperor had died on the 18 February

at the venerable age of seventy-nine, and after a record reign of thirty-four years. His most significant achievements had been the conquest of the southern Sung empire in 1279, followed by the reunification of China under a single, albeit foreign, ruler after almost four centuries of disunion.

To win over the Chinese Kublai had at an early stage adopted many of their customs and traditions, displaying a political insight which earned him the title of Sechen, 'the Wise'. He called his dynasty by the Chinese name of Ta-Yüan or Great Origin, and began reckoning the years of his reign according to the Chinese practice of reign-titles. Perhaps the most concrete symbol of the unification of his vast realm was the 1,200-mile-long Imperial Canal, which during his reign was extended to connect the seat of Mongol power in north China with Hangchow, the former Sung capital in the south.

Already during Möngke's reign Kublai had shown an unusual interest in foreign countries and especially China, so much so that he had even been accused by his relatives of being a sinophile. After his election he had not returned to remote Karakorum, but had settled in China for good, in the former capital of the Chin kingdom which had been badly damaged during the war with the Mongols in 1215. Kublai had Peking completely rebuilt by a Moslem architect slightly to the northeast, and on a grand and lavish scale. He added many new halls and palaces, artificial hills and lakes, and parks filled with game for the imperial hunt. Peking's reconstruction took more than ten years and Marco Polo, who has left a vivid description of it, saw it for the first time barely a year after it had been completed (1275).

Kublai renamed the city Daidu which was the Mongol pronunciation of Ta-tu, meaning in Chinese 'Great Capital'. However, among the Turkish and Persian-speaking people of Asia Peking had been known for a long time as Khanbaliq or Royal City, and this is also the name used by European travellers, including Marco Polo, Montecorvino, Odoric of Pordenone and John of Marignolli. Modern Peking dates only from the beginning of the fifteenth century and does not coincide exactly with the former Mongol capital, which extended farther to the north and less to the south than the present city.

Kublai's summer residence was at Shang-tu, the Ciandu of Marco Polo and the Xanadu of Coleridge, some 225 miles northwest of Peking. As the election of the new emperor in May 1294 took place in Shang-tu, John, who travelled as an official envoy, must have proceeded there without delay.

Temür Öljeitü ('the Fortunate'), thirty-year-old grandson of Kublai, was enthroned as Great Khan. John delivered to him the letters that Pope Nicholas had written to the deceased emperor and obtained permission to settle in the capital and carry out his religious work. As ambassador of the country of the Franks (for this is how he was regarded by the Mongol government) John enjoyed considerable status, and this was further enhanced by his dignity as Christian cleric. Moreover, he also benefited from the good relations then existing between the Mongols and Europe, and the patronage that Kublai had accorded other Westerners, notably the Polos, only a few years earlier.

THE CONVERSION OF PRINCE GEORGE OF TENDUC

John's primary concern was the spread of the Catholic faith in the dominion of the Great Khan. Towards the end of the thirteenth century there were in China many thousands of Christians of the Greek rite, found mainly among the Alan, Georgian and Russian troops serving in the imperial army. There were also numerous Christian Armenians, engaged in trade and various crafts. However, the Nestorians represented by far the largest and most powerful group. Nestorianism had not come to China with the Mongols but had been introduced as early as the middle of the seventh century by Syrian missionaries. The 'Brilliant Teaching', as this faith was then called in China, had flourished as a minor foreign religion until A.D. 845, when a fierce persecution directed against Buddhism and all foreign cults swept away the Church and its followers. During the Liao and Chin dynasties Nestorianism had reappeared in north China, brought by immigrants from Central Asia and Mongolia. The Mongol invasion gave a powerful boost to the Nestorian Church and we know from William of Rubruck that at the time (1254) the Nestorian Christians were established in fifteen cities. Twenty years later Marco Polo found Nestorian communities in the Yangtze region and even in Yünnan.

Kublai had embraced Buddhism under the influence of his wife Chabui and his Tibetan adviser Phagspa, but pursuing the liberal policy of his predecessors he had protected all the religions represented in his multi-national empire. The Nestorian clergy enjoyed the same tax exemption privileges and grain donations granted to the Buddhists, the Taoists and the Moslems, and a special government department for the Christian Cult was established by Kublai in 1289. Moreover, many important offices in the administration were held by Nestorian Turks. Already very influential through its connection with the Mongol court, the Nestorian Church in China grew even stronger after it resumed contact with its centres in Persia and Mesopotamia as a result of Mar Yahballaha's election to the patriarchal see.

Mar Yahballaha, as we have seen, originally came from the Öngüt country or, as Marco calls it, 'the country of Tenduc' (from the old Chinese name of this region). Now, when Montecorvino arrived in China, Khanbaliq was the seat of the Nestorian Archbishop, but the actual stronghold of Nestorianism was still the Öngüt territory. The flourishing state of Nestorianism in Tenduc is not only attested by contemporary Chinese and Western sources, but also by a large number of Christian relics that have come to light in recent decades. These include gravestones with crosses in relief, brass medals with St. George killing the dragon, and several hundred small bronze crosses which were used as amulets and seals, some of them bearing also symbolic doves and fishes. Moreover, the modern descendants of the Öngüt Christians were discovered in 1933 in the Erküt clan of the Ordos Mongols by the Belgian missionary Antoine Mostaert C.I.C.M.

The ruler of Tenduc was a certain Prince George, whom Marco Polo calls the sixth in descent from Prester John. This erroneous identification was due, as mentioned earlier, to an original confusion of names, but the error took root because Prince George had also the unique distinction in the East of being both a ruler and a Christian, a characteristic tradition-ally ascribed to Prester John.

John of Montecorvino, who must have learned about the existence of Prince George when he was still in Persia, and probably from Mar Yahballaha himself, also believed that he was a scion of the legendary king of the Indies. He was, therefore, eager to meet this exalted personage and attempt to convert him to Catholicism. He was well aware that Prince George was the son-in-law of the Great Khan, and obviously hoped that his conversion would be followed by that of other Mongol leaders.

As an official envoy John not only drew a generous stipend from the Mongol government, but he also enjoyed the privi-lege denied to the ordinary citizen of travelling freely on the state post-relay system. Thus, shortly after presenting his credentials to Temür, our friar left for the capital of Tenduc, which was some ten miles north of the present Pailingmiao in Inner Mongolia. Its ruins are now called Olon Süme ('Many Temples') by the native Mongols.

Prince George welcomed the papal legate and within a short time he renounced his Nestorian faith and embraced Catholicism, and was followed by many of his subjects. A church dedicated to the Trinity was immediately erected, probably under John's supervision. It had a cruciform foundation and was covered with beautiful glazed tiles bearing a blue Gothic leaf pattern, fragments of which can still be admired at the Musée Guimet in Paris.

The sincerity of Prince George's conversion is evidenced by his acceptance of the minor orders of the Roman Church, and by his naming his son John in honour of Montecorvino. This we know from John's own report. However, recent research has shown that Prince George was also a keen Confucian. This is not surprising since many Nestorians living in China had by then become sinicized in language as well as in customs. Clearly Prince George, like the Jesuits at the Peking court in the seventeenth century, did not regard these two doctrines as mutually exclusive.

JOHN OF MONTECORVINO'S LABOURS IN KHANBALIQ AND HIS APPOINTMENT AS ARCHBISHOP

The extraordinary success of John of Montecorvino in Tenduc was, unfortunately, very brief. Three years later, in 1298, Prince George died and with him perished the first and last Catholic ruler of the Far East. The Nestorian clergy, who had been bitterly opposed to the prince's 'apostasy', led the people of Tenduc back to their original faith and eradicated Catholicism from the land. Only the ruins of the Roman church of Olon Süme, discovered by Japanese archaeologists before World War II, still bear testimony to Montecorvino's work.

John's direct attempt to convert the Great Khan failed because, as he later wrote, Temür had already 'grown too old in idolatry'. By idolatry is meant Buddhism which Temür, like his grandfather, is known to have favoured. Frustrated in his efforts to win over the Mongol court, the Franciscan missionary concentrated his activity on the schismatic Christians living in Khanbaliq, among whom the Alans figured prominently. These were the descendants of the people of the Caucasus who half a century earlier had been deported by the Mongols to serve in their armies. In Kublai's time the Alan corps had played a leading part in the conquest of the Sung empire. They still professed Christianity (of the Greek rite), but being cut off from their original country and lacking a clergy, they welcomed John of Montecorvino as their pastor. The Alans, like all other Christians in China, were antagonized by the Nestorians and this, no doubt, must have strengthened the bond between them and the Catholic priest.

Subsequently John also attracted many Armenians, to whom he could preach in their own tongue. Many years of missionary work in the East had taught John the importance of learning foreign languages. On his arrival in China the friar, who already knew Armenian and Persian, acquired a knowledge of either Mongolian or Turkish, the two languages of the ruling élite. It was in one of these two idioms, but more likely in Turkish, that he soon after translated the Gospel and the Psalms. This translation is unfortunately lost, but it may reappear one day like so many documents of this period which have been discovered since the beginning of this century in China and in Central Asia.

John built two churches in Khanbaliq, one with a bell-tower, and the other only 'at a stone's throw' from the imperial palace. Peter of Lucalongo, whose business in China must have been successful, purchased the land on which the second church was built near the present Hsin-hua Men. Earlier, John had bought forty slave boys, presumably Chinese, whom he had baptized and instructed, and whom he had trained to sing the liturgy in Latin. From his palace Temür enjoyed listening to the boys chanting in the oratory nearby, happy in the thought that they were praying to Heaven and chanting benedictions for the prosperity of the imperial family.

In the first twelve years of his ministry John of Montecorvino claims to have baptized about six thousand people, adding that had it not been for the Nestorians he would have baptized 'more than thirty thousand'. The Nestorian clergy, jealous of their privileged position, naturally resented the intrusion of a Western cleric who claimed to be the sole representative of true Christianity. They feared that his superior knowledge of theology and liturgy would win over more of their followers in the capital. They began to spread damaging rumours about him, and went so far as to accuse him of being an impostor who had killed the true envoy of the Franks and seized the rich gifts that he was bringing to the Mongol emperor. At one point their intrigues almost landed the friar in gaol. In the end John was able to clear himself, but the opposition of the Nestorians remained one of the major obstacles to the spread of the Catholic doctrine. By the time John of Montecorvino died in 1328 his conversions probably did not exceed ten thousand. It is significant that in the administrative documents of the Yüan dynasty, many of which are extant, the Catholics are not distinguished by a special name from the Nestorians. The term designating the Nestorian clergy (*erke'üd*) covered also the Roman and

Eastern Christians. This clearly indicates that the Mongol government regarded Catholicism as a variety of Nestorianism not important enough to warrant a separate designation, a fact which may well account for the almost excessive resentment towards the Nestorians that we find in the letters and reports of the Franciscan mission.

It is almost certain that most, if not all, of these conversions were carried out among the schismatic Christians and the 'foreign' residents. The Europeans and Central and Western Asians living in China formed a special group in society in between the Mongol ruling class and the Chinese subjects. They served the Mongols as government officials and engaged in lucrative professions. The Mongols on the whole distrusted the Chinese and, lacking administrative and commercial skills, preferred to employ foreigners like Marco Polo for positions that carried responsibility. John also belonged to this privileged class, and like Marco was isolated from the bulk of the Chinese population by a social as well as by a language barrier. He obviously thought that if he succeeded in converting the élite the rest of the country would automatically follow. This may explain why neither he nor the friars who came after him apparently took the trouble to learn Chinese, and in their relations with the native population were forced to rely on interpreters. We know from John of Montecorvino himself that the scenes from the Bible painted in his church bore inscriptions in Latin, Turkish or Mongolian, and Persian 'so that all tongues may be able to read'. Chinese, the language of the majority of the inhabitants of Khanbaliq, was not included.

The difficulties encountered by the Franciscan in his evangelic work are reflected in his own statement that he was 'without confession' for eleven years. This means, of course, that in all this time he was not able to convert a single priest. In 1304 the lonely missionary was joined by another Minorite, Friar Arnold of Cologne, but he was still totally cut off from his Order, and in Europe he had actually been given up for dead.

News of his life and labours in China finally reached the West in 1306–7, when two letters that he had written to his confrères in Crimea and to the Minorites and Preachers of Persia were forwarded to the Curia. The second letter was personally delivered to Pope Clement V (1305–14) in Poitiers by the future martyr of Thana, Thomas of Tolentino, who also eloquently supported John of Montecorvino's plea for more helpers.

John's letters and Thomas's own intervention had the desired effect. Clement immediately created John of Montecorvino first Archbishop of Khanbaliq and Patriarch of the Orient, with jurisdiction over the whole Tartar empire from Kipchak and Asia Minor to Cathay. The pope also appointed seven other Franciscans as suffragan bishops and sent them to China in 1307 to consecrate John. Only three of them eventually reached the Mongol capital in 1313.

With their help Montecorvino decided to extend his missionary activity to the southern provinces of China, the 'Mangi' of Marco Polo, choosing Zaiton as the first episcopal seat. This city on the coast of Fukien near the present Amoy was the main port and trading centre in China from the eleventh to the fourteenth century. It was also the home of a thriving colony of foreign merchants. Both Marco Polo and the famous Arab traveller Ibn Battuta (1304–77/78) have left interesting descriptions of it. One of the most important Chinese geographical accounts of foreign countries was written in 1225 by a maritime inspector of Zaiton chiefly on the basis of information collected from sailors and merchants.

The Moslem, largely Persian, community was prominent

in Zaiton and its members worshipped in the local mosque, the oldest and most beautiful in China. Buddhism, Manicheism, Brahmanism and Nestorian Christianity had also numerous adherents, judging by the great number of inscribed tombstones that have been discovered in the city in the last twenty years.

FRIARS PEREGRINE OF CASTELLO AND ANDREW OF PERUGIA IN ZAITON

In 1313, or soon after, Friar Gerard Albuini was appointed first bishop of Zaiton. He was succeeded by Peregrine of Castello in 1318. Shortly after his appointment Friar Peregrine wrote a letter to his confrères in the Vicariate of the East which, together with the two letters of John of Montecorvino and the letter of Andrew of Perugia, is one of the few extant documents of the early Franciscan mission in China. For a long time this letter was regarded as spurious as it was not known to the Franciscan historian Luke Wadding (1588–1657), and was found in a manuscript which had belonged to a notorious forger. Although some doubts still subsist the letter is now generally accepted as genuine.

In it Friar Peregrine describes the Archbishop's life in the capital and his increasing success among the Armenians and Alans. In Zaiton, too, the friars carried out their apostolate chiefly among the local Christians. The church and convent had been donated by a wealthy Armenian lady who had also 'assigned the necessities of life for us and for others if they come'. In addition the friars had outside the city 'a beautiful place with a grove where we wish to build cells and an oratory.'

The same impression of material welfare is conveyed by Friar Andrew of Perugia, who succeeded Peregrine as bishop of Zaiton in 1322. In a letter he wrote in 1326 Friar Andrew described the comfortable state of the Franciscans in China. They continued to enjoy the generous imperial grant which 'exceeds the income and expenditure of many Western kings', and which, in the case of Andrew, amounted to a hundred golden florins a year. The friar's image of China and its ruler echoes the earlier description of Marco Polo: 'I forbear to speak of the wealth and magnificence and glory of this great emperor, of the vastness of the empire and the number of its cities and their size, and of the government of the empire, in which no man dares to draw sword against another; for it would be too long to write and would seem unbelievable to my hearers. For even I who am on the spot hear such things as I can hardly believe.'

Both Peregrine and Andrew refer in their letters to the Latin and Genoese merchants. There must have been quite a few of them in China, trading in gems, silk and spices, and practising other professions. Already John of Montecorvino, in his first letter from Khanbaliq, had mentioned the arrival in 1303 of a Lombard surgeon who had 'infected these parts with incredible blasphemies about the Roman Curia and our Order and the state of the West'. This otherwise unknown traveller, perhaps a heretic as many Lombards still were at the time, must have given John his own version of the struggle between Boniface VIII (1294–1303) and Philip the Fair, than at its height. The flow of Latin traders to China continued in the following decades. It seems that these merchants used the Catholic mission as a base, thus carrying on in the Far East that traditional association between mercantile and religious interests which existed in the Golden Horde and in Persia. When John of Marignolli visited Zaiton in 1346 the Franciscans owned a *fondaco*, i.e. an inn and warehouse, for the use of the Western merchants.

In his letter Andrew mentions also the freedom of cult in China, the friars' failure to convert Jews and Moslems, and the fact that although many Chinese had received baptism, they 'do not adhere strictly to Christian ways'. It is, indeed, doubtful how much of the Christian message reached the Chinese converts, as according to Friar Peregrine the missionaries preached to them through the intermediary of two interpreters.

In the last years of his life John of Montecorvino spent most of his time catering to the spiritual needs of the Armenian community in Khanbaliq, for whom he built another church, leaving the care of the other two churches to his coadjutors.

The Situation in China and the Buddhist Clergy

The Great Khan Temür Öljeitü had died in 1307 at the age of forty-two. Between 1307 and 1328, the year in which Montecorvino died, four emperors occupied the throne at Khanbaliq, their reigns marred and prematurely shortened by palace dramas and political assassinations. The government steadily deteriorated and the Chinese grew increasingly resentful of their oppressive foreign masters. In spite of certain concessions, such as the re-introduction in 1313 of the examination system and a mild promotion of the cult of Confucius, the court and the Mongol aristocracy did not basically change their attitude, regarding China only as a source of revenue.

The abuses of the Buddhist clergy, who after the conversion of Kublai had enjoyed the special favour of the Mongol emperors, were largely responsible for the widespread feeling of discontent among the people. As indicated earlier, the Mongol rulers had shown a predilection for Tibetan Tantric Buddhism. Its appeal lay perhaps less in the vast Mahayanic conception of salvation for all than in the astonishing feats of the Tibetan magicians who by all accounts were greatly superior to the native Mongol shamans. Marco Polo, who witnessed some of their performances at court, says that 'they know devilish arts and enchantments more than all other men, and control the devils, so that I do not believe there are greater charmers in the world.' One of their *pièces de résistance* was to cause cups full of wine to fly across the air to the emperor's table.

Besides impressing their masters with their divining powers and high-grade sorcery, the Tibetan priests proclaimed that the Mongol emperors were the reincarnations of the kings of Tibet and India, and in this way they traced their lineage to the Heavenly Buddhas. This was of course particularly flattering to the khans, as it confirmed their traditional claim to a divine origin. It is not surprising, then, that lamas from Tibet were soon appointed as Imperial Preceptors, a position that gave them control over all the Buddhist clergy in China. The first lama to hold this office was Phagspa 'the Holy' (*d.* 1279/80), who has also passed into history as the creator of a versatile new script, based on the Tibetan alphabet, which under Kublai became the official script of the Mongol government. After 1324 Phagspa became an object of veneration in all the temples of the empire.

Through the lamas' influence huge grants of money and land were lavished on the temples and the Buddhist clergy became involved in all sorts of extortion and illegal practices. Before long the Buddhist Church had become virtually a state within the state. Much of the wealth accumulated by the temples, of which there were 42,318 in 1291, flowed out of the country. According to a Chinese official writing at the beginning of the fourteenth century, half the annual national income went to Tibet. In 1322 when copper for coins was becoming scarce, a colossal 300-ton statue of Buddha was cast at a temple west of Khanbaliq, and this was by no means an isolated case. No amount of edicts conferring posthumous honours on Confucius and his disciples could redress the serious economic imbalance caused by such a policy.

In the few extant letters of the Franciscans of Cathay we would look in vain for references to the situation in the country, the influential role of the Tibetan lamas and the abuses of the Buddhist clergy. The friars were not blind to these facts and knew the true state of affairs but, prudently, refrained in their writings from criticising the court that protected them and the all-powerful Buddhist hierarchy. Nevertheless, some of the information that they had gathered on the subject reached Persia and found its way into the so-called *Book of the Estate of the Great Khan* written about 1330 by the Dominican John of Cori, Archbishop of Sultanieh.

We may recall that in 1318 Pope John XXII, in an effort to rationalize and strengthen the apostolate in the Orient after the conversion of the khans of the Golden Horde and Persia to the Islamic faith, had divided the missionary work in Asia between the Franciscan and Dominican Orders. The Minorites were entrusted with the three vicariates of Northern and Eastern Tartary and Cathay, i.e. the Near East, the Golden Horde, Mongolia and China, all of them depending upon the archdiocese of Khanbaliq. The Preachers were given jurisdiction over the dominion of the Ilkhans, Central Asia and India, their missions being under the authority of the archdiocese of Sultanieh (southeast of Tabriz), which since 1307 had become the Ilkhanids' capital. This redistribution also placed the Franciscan friaries in Persia under the authority of the Dominican Order.

In 1329 John of Cori, who in earlier days had served under John of Montecorvino in Persia, was appointed third arch-

5. Mongol ruler with his consort, ladies and attendants, from a fourteenth-century Persian manuscript.

6. Odoric of Pordenone, bas-relief by Filippo De Sanctis, 1332. Chiesa de Carmine, Udine.

bishop of Sultanieh. In his position he had access to all the information reaching Persia from Cathay through the Central Asian and southern sea routes. It was largely on the basis of this information, much of it proceeding from the Franciscan mission, that Archbishop John compiled his report which has fortunately come down to us.

After a description of the wealth of the Great Khan the author mentions the Buddhist Church in China with its temples and monks, and its 'sovereign bishop, such as the Pope is with us'. His authority is so great that the emperor 'honours him above all other men, and when the emperor rides in his company he makes him ride close by his side.' This Grand Priest 'has always the head and the beard shaven and wears on his head a red hat, and is always clothed in red.' All this is accurate, for we know from the Chinese sources that the Imperial Preceptors always sat next to the Great Khan at all official functions. The red hat and robes were the distinctive garments of the Tantric sects.

John of Cori's account also contains interesting information on the post-relay system, the ethnography of China and the activity of the Franciscans. It is from him that we learn about the death of John of Montecorvino, who had passed away in the Mongol capital two years before at the age of eighty-one, mourned by 'a very great multitude of Christian people and of pagans'.

The first archbishop of Khanbaliq had no real successor. Andrew of Perugia, who by his own statement was still active and well in 1326, died, apparently, only six years later. A tombstone with a cross on top, two angels in relief and a Latin inscription, discovered recently in Chüanchow, has been identified by J. Foster as being that of Friar Andrew. According to this scholar the almost illegible date at the end of the inscription probably represents 1332.

The third bishop of Zaiton also had no successor. In his letter of 1326 Andrew remarked that of the seven suffragan bishops sent to China by Pope Clement he was the only one still alive. The Franciscan sources speak of three other bishops appointed in 1310–11 by Clement, but nothing is known about them except their names.

On the other hand there were several Minorites in China about whom the official records are silent. They were sent by John of Montecorvino to establish churches and convents in other important centres of China, notably Hangchow in Chekiang and Yangchow in Kiangsu. Our knowledge of these missions comes from the memoirs of the celebrated friar and traveller Odoric of Pordenone, who spent several years in China in the 1320's.

IX

Odoric, the Roving Friar

The story of Odoric's journey as related by himself is one of the most extraordinary pieces of travel literature that exist. Odoric's fame as a missionary and even as a saint—he was beatified in 1755—is eclipsed by his travels in Asia and the controversy to which they gave rise.

There has been a good deal of speculation about his life, the bare facts of which can be reconstructed as follows. He was born, probably between 1265 and 1286, in the Mattiussi family of Villanova near the town of Pordenone in Friuli. In his youth he joined the Franciscan Order and spent several years practising severe asceticism in his native province. Before 1320 he left for the East with one companion, Friar James of Ireland, and a servant 'in order to win some harvest of souls'.

The party sailed to Constantinople and Trebizond, and proceeded from there to Sultanieh via Erzerum and Tabriz. Odoric's itinerary then becomes somewhat confused and he seems to have wandered from place to place in Persia and Mesopotamia, visiting Kashan, Yezd, Persepolis and Baghdad, before embarking for India at Hormuz. He was at Thana on the island of Salsette near Bombay in 1321 or 1322, shortly after the slaughter of four Franciscan friars who had gone there to establish a Catholic mission on the Malabar coast. One of these martyrs was Thomas of Tolentino, already mentioned in connection with John of Montecorvino's appointment. Odoric took their bones with him to China. Before leaving India he visited the Church of St. Thomas at Mylapore.

On his eastward voyage the friar touched Sumatra, Java and Champa (South Vietnam). He reached Canton, in 'the noble province of Manzi, which we call Upper India', sometime in 1322–23. Odoric's 'Manzi' is the 'Mangi' of Marco Polo and the popular designation in the thirteenth and fourteenth centuries of southern China, whereas 'Cathay' usually refers to the north. It derived from a contemptuous term used originally by the northern Chinese for the people living in the southern provinces. Because of its situation in the south, Manzi was regarded as an extension of India by Odoric and other contemporary travellers.

From Canton Odoric and his companion travelled by land to Zaiton, Fuchow, Hangchow, Nanking and Yangchow. From Yangchow they proceeded to Khanbaliq by the Grand Canal. They arrived at the Mongol capital in about 1325 and remained there for three years. They then returned to the West through north China, Central Asia and Persia. Back in Italy in 1330 Odoric dictated his memoirs in the Convent of St. Anthony at Padua. Soon after, he set off to Avignon in order to obtain permission from the pope to return to China with a group of missionaries, but he was overcome by sickness on the way and returned to Udine, where he died on 14 January 1331. These last two dates are the only reliable ones of his entire biography.

It is still doubtful whether Odoric set out from Italy with the idea of going as far as China. It seems more likely that he was brought there by fortuitous circumstances and prompted, we feel, as much by his adventurous spirit as by religious zeal.

His travelogue, which has come down to us in a great number of manuscript copies—alas, not without many interpolations—resembles more an old-fashioned tourist guide than a missionary's report, but this is precisely what makes it so valuable and interesting. Odoric's narrative has in fact preserved many colourful stories, legends and sundry anecdotes about peoples and places that travellers in the East picked up from local *ciceroni* and story-tellers, as well as from other travellers. These the naïve and somewhat gullible friar usually passes off as genuine, sometimes even giving the impression of having been himself a witness. In his report we find references to gold and silver palaces, dog-faced men, magic stones and other tales also related by Marco Polo, with whose account he was certainly familiar.

One of the most interesting stories told by Odoric concerns his visit to a Buddhist monastery in Hangchow (Cansai, the Quinsai of Marco Polo) where he witnessed an extraordinary show. His Chinese host beat upon a gong and from the hill nearby came a multitude of animals 'such as apes, monkeys and many other animals having faces like men'. They took places around him and, after having been fed, went back to their retreats. Friar Odoric marvelled at this unusual performance, but his host explained to him that souls of human beings dwelt in the bodies of these animals, hence their response to his call.

Now from the Chinese sources we know that this story was current in Hangchow in the time of Odoric, but its hero was a monk of the eighth century A.D. who, in the same monastery, used to keep apes which he could summon by whistling. There were, however, no monkeys there in the fourteenth century. Odoric visited the temple and heard the story, and may have even seen some other animals fed in the temple gardens. Later the popular anecdote and his actual experience were conflated in his recollection of the event.

In his description of Hangchow, 'the greatest and noblest city, and the finest for merchandise, that the world contains', Odoric mentions in a rather cursory way the presence of Minorites, four of whom had converted a local high official.

In Yangchow, which he visited on his way north, the friar noted a Franciscan convent and 'three churches of the Nestorians'. The existence in this city of a Catholic community was confirmed by the chance discovery in 1951 of the most important Christian relic in China. This is the famous tombstone of Catherine, daughter of the Venetian merchant Dominic Vilioni, who died in Yangchow in 1342. The stone, inscribed in Old Gothic letters, is decorated with beautiful vignettes showing the martyrdom of St. Catherine of Alexandria, the translation of her body, and two angels flying towards a Madonna and Child. The Chinese style of these scenes indicates that the sculpture was executed by a local artist.

The Venetian merchant family of Vilioni had settled in Persia in the thirteenth century and from there some of its members must have later migrated to Yangchow. Marco Polo himself spent three years in this city, apparently as an official of the Salt Administration. It seems likely, then, that there was in Yangchow a small colony of Venetians engaged in trade and with their own church run by Franciscan friars. Catherine Vilioni is the only European woman known to have lived and died in China before the nineteenth century.

Odoric's description of Khanbaliq is of great interest since it adds to our knowledge of the imperial city and is a valuable complement to Marco Polo's account. Odoric was not a papal envoy and did not carry any credentials, but he shared in the privileges conferred by the Mongol government on his confrères. With them he participated in the religious ceremonies for the emperor 'because we Brothers Minor have a place appointed us in his court and must always go and give him our blessing.'

It was customary, whenever one met the Great Khan, to have something ready to offer him. Odoric reports how, on one occasion, he and his companions took some apples and offered them to the emperor on a dish: 'And he took two of the apples and ate a little of one. And then our bishop aforesaid (i.e. John of Montecorvino) gave him his blessing. And this done he signed to us to retire lest the horses coming after him and the crowd should hurt us in any way.'

Odoric has much to say about the imperial palaces, the entertainments at court, the emperor's grandiose hunts and how the Great Khan travelled across the land 'with four armies of horsemen, one of which goes a day's march in front of him, one at each side, and one a day's march in the rear, so that he goes always, as it were, in the middle of a cross.'

Often a keener observer than Marco Polo, Odoric is the first Westerner to mention the Chinese custom of binding women's feet, the long nails of the Chinese gentlemen, and the curious method of fishing with the cormorant, which was later introduced into Europe, these versatile birds being trained to catch fish and disgorge them into their owner's boat.

From Odoric we also learn about native varieties of fowl, of which our friar not only gives the first accurate description, but also the current market price. Such detailed information on the material culture of the Chinese contrasts sharply with an almost complete silence on his missionary work. He does not mention even once by name any of the other Minorites with whom he lived and worked for three years. Odoric's presence in China is itself likewise ignored

by Andrew of Perugia in his letter of 1326. This is difficult
to understand, particularly as Odoric during his stay at
Zaiton had deposited in the local friary the remains of the
four Thana martyrs. The martyrdom of these Franciscans
is mentioned in Andrew's letter, but Odoric's name does
not appear.

We know that in the second half of the thirteenth and in
the early fourteenth century the Franciscan Order had been
torn by a bitter conflict between the Spirituals and the
Community. The Spirituals, formerly called Zealots, wished
to preserve the features of primitive Franciscan life and
insisted on absolute poverty. The Community, on the other
hand, stood for a less rigid observance of poverty and a more
organized form of apostolate. John of Montecorvino probably
belonged to the Spirituals, many of whom were found
among the friars active in the Orient, especially in Armenia.
Now in Bishop Andrew's letter there is a definite hint at
some disagreement between him and his superior in Khanbaliq, the nature of which is not specified. This fact and
Andrew's silence over Odoric's visit compel us to ask
whether the internal conflict of the Order had also made
itself felt among the Franciscans in China. Odoric's leanings
in the controversy are a matter of speculation; it is worth
noting, however, that Pope John XXII's bulls against the
Spirituals were issued in 1317–20, i.e. just before our friar
undertook his long journey to the East.

On his return journey Odoric passed through Tenduc and
the country of Prester John. His first comment is that 'not
one hundredth part is true of what is told of him.' This
reminds us of Marco Polo's remark that perhaps only one
tenth of what they tell about 'King John' corresponds to
reality. The friar compares the capital of Tenduc with the
town of Vicenza in northern Italy, to the disadvantage of the

former, and recalls the marriage agreement between King John and the Great Khan which is also mentioned by Marco.

Odoric is the last Western traveller to refer to Prester John as an Asiatic ruler. The sobering accounts of the thirteenth century travellers, and their failure to meet a Christian ruler whose power and wealth resembled that of the traditional potentate, brought to an end the Asiatic cycle of the myth. After the second decade of the fourteenth century the legend of Prester John was transferred to Ethiopia. This country was wealthy, mysterious, ruled by a Christian dynasty, and the Ethiopians had occasionally fought the Moslems. There was also, as we have seen, an early association between Prester John and the king of Ethiopia which went back to the Fifth Crusade. Added to this was the perennial confusion between Ethiopia and India, the political and religious authority held by the rulers of Ethiopia, and the fact that they bore the title of *zān* ('king'), which had a strong resemblance to the name John. All these factors combined to make the new myth acceptable in the West, where it enjoyed great popularity for two more centuries, stimulating fresh explorations and adventurous journeys in search of the fabulous monarch.

Odoric crossed Tenduc on his way to Kansu (Tangut) and Central Asia. Travelling through this region he collected sundry bits of information about Tibet, such as the way the Tibetans dispose of their dead by hacking them to pieces and letting the vultures feed on them. It is doubtful whether he personally visited this country as he claims in his book. Odoric's itinerary from Kansu onwards is not known. He probably took the southern caravan route through Khotan and Kashgar, and gained the Near East by way of Persia.

Odoric's narrative became immensely popular in Italy and abroad. However, like Marco Polo, the peripatetic friar met with incredulity and worse. In England Samuel Purchas accused him of plagiarizing Sir John Mandeville, and as late as the middle of the eighteenth century the editor of *Astley's Collection of Voyages* still referred to him as 'a great liar'. This injustice was later redressed, and we owe to the loving labour and scholarship of another Englishman, Sir Henry Yule (1820–89), the first critical edition and translation of Odoric's *Travels*, which is still indispensable today.

Odoric left China before the death of John of Montecorvino. Although the passing away of Montecorvino is mentioned in John of Cori's *Book of the Estate of the Great Khan* of 1330, the papal court at Avignon was not informed about it until 1333. In September of that year John XXII appointed a new Archbishop of Khanbaliq in the person of a certain Friar Nicholas. This obscure Minorite departed for the East in the following year endowed with wide powers and numerous papal letters, including one for the ruler of Korea. He seems to have got as far as Almaliq (near modern Kulja in Sinkiang), where the Franciscans had a suffragan see depending from Khanbaliq, but it is almost certain that he never reached China, and his fate and that of his companions is unknown.

Well documented, on the other hand, is the mission of John of Marignolli (1338–53), whose journey to the Mongol court is both the culmination of Mongol-European contacts and the swan-song of the Christian mission to Cathay.

X

The Last Mission to Cathay

THE ALANS' PETITION

In 1336 several chiefs of the Christian Alans of Khanbaliq
wrote a petition to Pope Benedict XII (1334–42) requesting the appointment of a pontifical legate to China to succeed John of Montecorvino who had died there eight years
before.

The Alans' letter was taken to Avignon by an embassy
of the Great Khan Toghon Temür (1333–68), led by the
Genoese Andalò of Savignone, better known as Andrew the
Frank. Andrew carried also a letter from Toghon Temür
himself in which the emperor expressed his desire to open
the way for frequent diplomatic exchanges with the pope
'Lord of the Christians in Frankland beyond the seven seas
where the sun goes down'. He requested the pontiff to send
him his blessing and to remember him in his prayers, and
he recommended the Alans, 'his servants and Christian
sons'. He also asked the pope to send him horses and other
rarities from the West.

There has been much discussion in the past on the real
purpose of this mission, particularly in view of the emperor's
request for the papal blessing. Some scholars, knowing that
Toghon Temür was a fervent devotee of Tantrism, found
such a request incongruous and cast doubts on the authenticity of the letter. These doubts, however, are not justified.

It is true that Toghon was a follower of Tibetan Buddhism, but like his forefathers he believed in the efficacy of prayers and benedictions of all religions, a fact amply confirmed by the texts of edicts issued to the various Churches of the empire during his reign.

His wish to obtain horses and other rarities calls for some comment. Since antiquity the Western lands had been regarded by the peoples of Asia as a source of rare and marvellous objects, just as the reverse was true. The Mongols, as a result of their conquests, had learned to appreciate the products of Europe; and at the time the request and despatch of gifts were, of course, an essential part of diplomatic exchanges. Gems of all kinds, embroidered cloth, and falcons for hunting were among the items most in demand at the Mongol court.

In a letter that Arghun sent to Edward I and Philip the Fair in 1289 through his ambassador Buscarello di Gisolfo (also a Genoese), the Ilkhan had asked the two Western monarchs to send him 'marvellous objects, gerfalcons and precious stones of different colour'. Two years later Arghun had sent as a present to Philip a *kulan*, or wild ass of the Asiatic steppe, which was as much a rarity in Europe as were the large northern European horses in the Far East.

In 1328–29 an embassy from an unidentified European country (there is no record of it in any Western source) had already brought a horse to the Great Khan at Khanbaliq. This unusual gift had caused a sensation at court and a Chinese scholar had written a poem to celebrate the event. It should be mentioned that the Chinese had for many centuries regarded the sturdier horses from the Western Regions, especially the Ferghana or Turkmen steeds, as the best in the world. Possession of these 'heavenly horses' or, as they were also called, 'blood-sweating horses', had become a concrete symbol of the emperor's universal rule. They had even acquired a magico-religious quality as the proper vehicle for the emperor's mystical journey to immortality, and were sacrificed in his tomb.

Now the Mongol emperors of the latter part of the dynasty had all been instructed in Chinese language and literature, and were no doubt familiar with the lore of the Heavenly Horse. As the pope was considered not only the political leader of the West, but also its leading thaumaturge, a gift of horses from him must have been regarded by Toghon Temür as a particularly valuable acquisition.

In their letter the Alan chiefs referred to the pope's former legate John of Montecorvino as 'a man of weighty, capable and holy character'. They asked for a person like him to be appointed as soon as possible 'to care for their souls', as the one whom they heard the pope had sent, i.e. Friar Nicholas, 'had never yet appeared.'

The Catholic community of Khanbaliq, largely represented by the Alans, had thus been for several years without a pastor. From the tone of their letter it is evident that the Alans were anxious to get one, partly, we may infer, to counter more effectively the opposition of the Nestorian clergy. The Alans, we must not forget, still formed the backbone of the Mongol army. The first signatory of the letter to the pope, Fodim Jovens, was the head of all Alans and the President of the Board of War. This fact gives, I think, the clue to the true reason for the Great Khan's embassy to the West. What prompted this mission perhaps was not so much Toghon Temür's wish to restore diplomatic relations with Europe or his interest in acquiring portentous horses, but rather his desire to please the military chiefs on whom depended the security of the state and the emperor's own safety.

This interpretation is all the more acceptable if we con-sider that when these events took place the unpopularity of the Mongol régime was nearing its peak because of the anti-Chinese policy of the prime minister Bayan. Bayan's dream was to wipe out all people bearing the surnames of Chang, Wang, Liu, Li and Chao, which correspond to our Smith, Jones and Brown. Fortunately, he was not allowed to carry out this scheme, but his repressive measures during the years he was in power (1333–40) hastened considerably the fall of the dynasty. Surrounded by a vast and hostile popula-tion, the ineffectual Mongol court could only rely for its survival on the support of its loyal troops.

Toghon Temür's embassy, which arrived at Avignon at the end of May 1338, included, along with Andrew the Frank, the Frenchman William of Nassio, an Alan called Toghai and various other officials. Significantly not one Mongol appears among the leaders of this mission, whose composition in fact highlights once more the important role played by the Italians in the diplomatic exchanges between the Mongol empire and Europe.

The ambassadors were received with great honours by the pope, who promised to appoint his own legates to Khan-baliq soon. After three weeks in Avignon the envoys left and slowly made their way to Genoa, where they boarded a ship for Naples. When they arrived there in March 1339 they were met by the papal embassy that had been appointed in the meantime by Benedict. This consisted of a large group of Minorites led by Nicholas Bonet, former Professor of Theology at the University of Paris, and John of Marignolli, a Florentine friar of aristocratic lineage. The Western lega-tion, besides numerous letters addressed to the Great Khan, the chief of the Alans and the Mongol princes of Asia, carried also the handsome papal gifts, including a number of great war-horses. King Robert of Anjou, who entertained the legation in Naples, added his own gifts for the Great Khan.

The joint embassies must have been quite an impressive sight when they left for Constantinople at the beginning of April. On arrival at the Byzantine capital Nicholas Bonet had to return to Europe for unknown reasons, and John of Marignolli took charge of the mission.

JOHN OF MARIGNOLLI'S JOURNEY TO CATHAY

Our knowledge of Marignolli's early life is very scanty. He came from a noble family of Florence which played an active part in the political and cultural life of the city until it died out at the beginning of the seventeenth century. Before his appointment as papal legate, Friar John had been a lecturer in Bologna.

The story of his journey to China is known only through his own account, which is embedded in a larger historical work that he compiled towards the end of his life and to which we shall return later.

From the Crimean port of Caffa (now Feodosiya) where it landed after crossing the Black Sea at the end of June, the mission proceeded by way of Tana to the court of Khan Özbeg at New Sarai. Özbeg (1313–41) was the last great ruler of the Golden Horde, which had by now become predominantly Turkish in culture and language, and Moslem in faith. In spite of occasional setbacks, the situation in the Horde compared still very favourably with that in Persia, where the conversion to Islam of the Mongol rulers had been followed by the persecution of Christian communities and the rapid decline of missionary activity. It was mainly as a consequence of these developments in Persia and

Mesopotamia that in the second quarter of the fourteenth century the Church had shifted much of its missionary work from Western Asia to Northern Tartary, a fact which also accounts for Marignolli's visit.

Friar John was welcomed by Özbeg to whom he delivered a papal letter inviting him to further diplomatic exchanges. Among the gifts that the legate presented to the khan there was also one of the famous horses.

Özbeg entertained the legation through the winter, and when the party left in the spring of 1340 he provided an escort as far as the city of Almaliq in Central Asia.

We are not told about the route followed by the Franciscans from the Volga region to eastern Sinkiang. If they took, as is likely, the regular commercial road described by Francesco Balducci Pegolotti in his manual of business practice, they must have crossed the Ural near Gurev, the town of Urgench (now Kunya-Urgench) south of the Aral, and Otrar, and probably arrived at Almaliq in the autumn. In Almaliq, capital of the Chaghataid domain, they learned of the massacre of the local Franciscan mission which had occurred only the year before. The Bishop of Almaliq and six friars had been the victims of a persecution launched by a fanatical Moslem usurper who had, in turn, perished shortly after.

Marignolli and his companions stayed in this town until late in 1341 and succeeded in rebuilding the church and the convent which had been destroyed during the persecution. They resumed their journey through East Turkestan but halted again at Qomul (Hami), where Marignolli spent some time preaching among the predominantly Buddhist population.

7. The Yangchow Latin tombstone of Catherine Vilioni, 1342.

8. Page from the so-called 'Bible of Marco Polo'. Thirteenth century.

AUDIENCE WITH TOGHON TEMÜR AND SOJOURN
AT KHANBALIQ

Progressing eastwards across the desert the papal embassy
reached the province of Tangut, crossed the country of
Tenduc (which Marignolli ignores completely in his account), and finally arrived at the residence of the Great
Khan. According to Marignolli, the meeting with Toghon
Temür took place at Khanbaliq, but it is more likely that
he saw the emperor at his summer residence of Shang-tu,
as the date of the audience recorded in the Chinese imperial
annals is 19 August 1342.

The legate later recalled the solemn event in these words:
'The Great Khan, when he saw the war-horses and the
pope's presents and the sealed letter and King Robert's too
with the gold and us, *rejoiced with great joy* [my italics] think-
ing all very good, indeed the best, and honoured us very
highly. Moreover when I was ceremonially dressed, with
a most beautiful cross which went before me with candles
and incense, singing *Credo in Unum Deum*, we entered into
the presence of the Kaan dwelling in the glorious palace.
And when the chant was ended I gave a full benediction
which he received with humility.'

In the above passage Marignolli describes the emperor's
rejoicing in identical terms as those used in the Bible for
the Wise Men when they perceived the star that guided
them to Bethlehem. One may gauge from it the importance
that the papal legate attached to his mission.

In sharp contrast to this rather florid description, the
Chinese annals merely note the gift of 'a remarkable horse'
from the Kingdom of the Franks which, the text says, was
eleven feet three inches long, six feet four inches high, the
body entirely black and the two hind hoofs both white.

The emperor was very pleased with the present from the pope. The court painter Chou Lang was immediately summoned and ordered to make a portrait of the horse with the emperor riding on it. This was completed in record time only two days later. Then the President of the Academy of Literature instructed the renowned scholar Ou-yang Hsüan (1283–1357) to compose a poem in honour of the equine marvel. Ou-yang Hsüan duly complied and soon after presented to the throne his 'Ode to the Heavenly Horse', which reads in part as follows:

> *The Son of Heaven is humane and sage*
> *and all nations have submitted to him.*
> *The Heavenly Horse has come*
> *from the west of the West.*
> *Dark clouds cover its body,*
> *it has two hoofs of jade.*
> *It is more than five feet high*
> *and twice as much in length.*
> *In crossing seven oceans*
> *its body seemed to fly.*
> *The seas were like its retinue*
> *and thunders followed by.*
> *When the Emperor was in the Hall*
> *of Goodness and Humanity, at daybreak,*
> *Suddenly the west wind rose*
> *and the Heavenly Horse appeared,*
> *With dragon head, and phoenix breast,*
> *and eyes that darted lightning.*

In this as in many other poems on the Heavenly Horse written by contemporary Chinese scholar-officials, the gift from the Western lands is represented as a tribute, both concrete and symbolic, to the enlightened and all-embracing rule of the Mongol sovereign. Neither the pope nor his envoy get even a passing mention. This amusing episode illustrates well the extent to which East and West in their relations were deceived by their own cultural biases.

Chou Lang's painting still existed in the imperial collection of the Manchu dynasty in the early nineteenth century, but is now unfortunately lost, probably destroyed during the burning of the Summer Palace by Lord Elgin in 1860.

The whole Western mission, comprising thirty-two persons, was entertained at the Mongol court in Khanbaliq for about three years, 'two princes being appointed who ministered to us most liberally in all necessities . . . always with infinite respect, honouring us and the retinue with costly clothing. And if I were to reckon it all exactly, he (the emperor) spent more than the value of 4000 marks for us.'

Marignolli has little to say about his life in Khanbaliq. He mentions only the churches built by the Franciscans, the generous treatment that they received from the emperor, and the good name left behind by John of Montecorvino 'whom the Alans venerate as a saint'.

During his stay in China Friar John had also 'many glorious disputations with the Jews and other sects'. He is the third, and last, European to mention the presence of Jews in Mongol-ruled China, the other two being Marco Polo and Andrew of Perugia. Unfortunately none of them states clearly where the Jews were mostly found. The Arabic traveller Ibn Battuta noted the existence of Jews in Hangchow, but it seems that there were also Jewish communities in Zaiton and Khanbaliq, and it is probably to the one in the capital that Marignolli alludes. From the fifteenth century onward the most flourishing Jewish community was at Kaifeng in Honan province. The Jews, like the Moslems and the Nestorian Christians, regarded the Catholics as the worst of idolaters because, as Marignolli explains, 'they abhor images, carved faces and alarmingly life-like sculptures such as there are in our churches.' Some, at least, of our friar's glorious disputations must have been on the subject of idolatry.

MARIGNOLLI'S TRAVELS IN ASIA AND HIS RETURN TO EUROPE

Pope Benedict had nominated Marignolli as his personal legate in the belief that Friar Nicholas, whom he had elected Archbishop of Khanbaliq, had in the meantime taken possession of his see. Marignolli does not mention Nicholas at all, and it is almost certain that he never reached the capital. Nevertheless Marignolli, who regarded himself merely as an ambassador, obviously did not wish to take his place and assume responsibility for the whole vicariate of Cathay, since after three years at Khanbaliq he decided to return to Europe, much against the emperor's wishes.

His decision to leave China may have also been prompted by concern over the rapidly deteriorating situation in the country. Pressure was certainly mounting, and the rebellion which in the end overthrew the Mongol régime erupted in 1348, less than three years after Marignolli's departure. Sporadic fighting in the provinces had already started in 1337.

Marignolli's patron, emperor Toghon Temür, is portrayed by the Chinese historians as a typical degenerate last emperor of a dynasty, selfishly indulging his whims and pleasures, and oblivious of the fate of his country and of his own house. One of his favourite pastimes, besides hunting, was to construct ingenious mechanical contrivances such as animated clocks, with human and animal dummies marking time, and sophisticated dragon boats. Later, through the pernicious influence of his minister Hama, a Kangli Turk, he became interested in Tibetan sexual mysticism and eventually gave himself completely to these esoteric practices. Rumours of the emperor's participation in collective sexual rituals spread outside the palace, causing great scandal among the puritanical Chinese, so that 'even people in the market hated to hear about them.'

Although all this happened after Marignolli had left China, the Franciscan must have become aware during his lengthy sojourn at court that Toghon was a lax and incompetent monarch, and that the tide of events in the country bode evil for the foreign rulers.

He left, carrying many presents, and bringing with him the Great Khan's request that either he or someone else of the Minorite Order be sent 'speedily back with the rank of Cardinal, and with full powers, to be Bishop there'.

The large convoy, which also comprised a 200-knight escort, crossed China lengthwise to reach the port of Zaiton, where Marignolli was to embark for India and the Persian Gulf. The overland route had just been cut off by a war in the Chaghataid dominion which split it into two separate khanates. The weakened structures of the Mongol empire were collapsing everywhere.

Crossing Manzi, 'which once used to be called Greatest India', Marignolli was impressed by its countless cities and towns, and in particular by Hangchow, whose buildings, temples 'where there are 1000 to 2000 monks living together', and 'noble bridges of stone' he describes in enthusiastic terms. He was not aware that most of those 'monks' were actually laymen who crowded the temples to evade taxes and compulsory labour, nor had he any doubts that the Buddhist 'Goddess of Mercy' Kuan-yin, worshipped in one of the local temples, was the Virgin Mother of the Messiah.

On the other hand, some of his remarks are interesting, e.g. when speaking of the New Year's festival in Hangchow, he correctly points out that the first month of the year in China corresponds to our February.

Of Zaiton 'a marvellous seaport and a city to us incredible', Marignolli recalls only the three churches built by his confrères and the already mentioned *fondaco*, which was used then as 'depository of all the merchants'. He stayed long enough in the city to have two bells cast. These he baptized Johannina and Antonina, and placed them, with characteristic Florentine spirit, right in the middle of the Moslem quarter. He sailed from Zaiton 'on the feast of St. Stephen' (26 December 1245), but we do not know how many of his former companions left with him.

The party arrived at Quilon in April of the following year. Marignolli contracted there acute dysentery and was detained fourteen months with the friars of the Dominican mission founded fifteen years before by the first bishop of India, Jordan Catalani of Sévérac. Jordan had built a church at Quilon dedicated to St. George which the papal legate adorned with many paintings during his stay.

From his confrères Marignolli must have learned a good deal about the St. Thomas Christians. He is, apparently, the first Western traveller to call them by this name. He decided to visit the Christian community of the Coromandel coast and the famous tomb of the Apostle. Earlier, on his voyage from China to Quilon, he had sailed past Cape Comorin. Now, the southernmost tip of the subcontinent was for the friar the extreme limit of the world. Realizing that his journey had thus taken him 'beyond the glory of Alexander the Great', on his way to Coromandel Marignolli stopped at Cape Comorin to erect a commemorative pillar with the pope's and his own arms engraved on it, and an inscription both in Indian and Latin characters 'intended to last till the world's end'. According to a popular legend Alexander had erected a column in India to mark the furthest point he had reached—a feat that the proud Florentine could not leave unchallenged!

Although he paid only a brief visit to the Church of St. Thomas and the Nestorian community of Mylapore 'in Lower India', Marignolli includes in his account many of the curious legends surrounding the Apostle and his tomb. One, with practical implications, is that relating to a perpetual grant, made by a local king to St. Thomas, of public steelyards to measure pepper and all other spices, a privilege that 'no one dares take from the Christians but at the risk of death'. The papal legate too, as a perquisite of his office, was able to draw a handsome allowance from it during his stay in India. From him we learn that the local Christians were at the time more numerous than the Moslems.

From Mylapore our indefatigable traveller set out to explore the Sunda Islands. He visited the East Javanese kingdom of Majapahit, then ruled by a queen, and was convinced that he had found the original kingdom of Sheba (Saba). There he was finally cured of his illness by the queen's female physician with 'certain juices of herbs and an abstinent diet'.

On his return voyage to India Marignolli's ship was hit by gales and forced to take shelter in a harbour of Ceylon, which he calls 'a glorious mountain opposite to Paradise' and 'the loftiest spot on the face of the earth'.

The Franciscan's fond recollection of the island is probably due to its association with the Terrestrial Paradise. He believed this to be only forty Italian miles from it, so that 'the sound of waters falling from the fountains of Paradise is heard there.' In his cosmological system the four rivers of

Paradise flowed through Ceylon before going in separate directions. Describing one of these rivers, the Gihon or Nile, Marignolli mentions for the first and only time the land of Prester John, which he unhesitatingly identifies with Ethiopia 'where are now the negroes'.

The learned friar's concept of the world is a peculiar blend of scriptural, historical and philosophical notions, all strongly coloured by his own interpretation of the human and physical geography of Asia. Perhaps its most salient feature is a conscious attempt at rationalizing unusual phenomena and traditionally accepted tales, such as those concerning the fabulous races of India. Of these Marignolli writes: 'The truth is that no such people do exist as nations, though there may be an individual monster here and there. Nor is there any people at all such as has been invented, who have but one foot which they use to shade themselves with. But as all the Indians commonly go naked, they are in the habit of carrying a thing like a little tent-roof on a cane handle, which they open out at will as a protection against sun or rain . . . and this is what the poets have converted into a foot.' He actually took an Indian umbrella with him to show it to the citizens of Florence.

Marignolli's paradisiacal island was not without its serpent. A local tyrant, who was also 'a eunuch and an accursed Saracen', cunningly stripped him of most of his money and all the valuable gifts of Toghon Temür, which included 'gold, silver, silk, cloth of gold, precious stones, pearls, camphor, musk, myrrh, and aromatic spices'. The friar and his companions were detained 'with all politeness' by this man for four months.

After his departure from Ceylon, we can still follow Marignolli from Hormuz to the Mediterranean through Baghdad, Mosul, Edessa, Aleppo, Damascus, Jerusalem and

Cyprus. He arrived in Avignon in 1353 with the Great Khan's letter, written eight years before, and much to report to the newly elected pope Innocent VI (1352–62).

In recognition of his services the Florentine cleric received fifty florins and the bishopric of Bisignano in Calabria. One may wonder whether Marignolli regarded this promotion as a reward or a punishment; at any rate he never took possession of his see. Shortly after the appointment he accepted an invitation of Emperor Charles IV to become his domestic chaplain and historiographer.

It was in this capacity that, during his stay at the royal court in Prague, Marignolli completed a *Chronicle of Bohemia*. The task was one that he found particularly distasteful because of the many strange names he had to contend with, names that with his Florentine tongue he could not even pronounce. As a diversion he interspersed the monotonous narrative with the recollections of his travels in Asia. He died, probably in Prague, in 1358 or 1359.

Marignolli's work fell into oblivion until 1768, when it was exhumed and published for the first time. Still no one noticed the interpolated passages until they were extracted from the chronicle and brought together by J. G. Meinert in 1820.

THE END OF THE CATHOLIC MISSIONS TO CATHAY

According to the Franciscan *Chronicle of the Twenty-four Generals*, compiled shortly after the death of Marignolli, the Great Khan in his letter to the pope had requested him to send more preachers to his empire. Marignolli, as we have seen, also mentions the emperor's wish for clerics of the Minorite Order. On receiving the legate's report, Innocent asked the Franciscan hierarchy to designate a number of missionaries, but no action was taken. The chronicler blames his Order for its lack of zeal in appointing a new mission. The real cause, however, was the bubonic plague, or Black Death, which in 1348 had almost emptied the Minorite convents in Europe (two-thirds of the friars had perished within a year), combined with a general decline of missionary activity in Asia as a result of persecutions and political anarchy.

In China the anti-Mongol rebellion had gathered momentum after 1356. In the following years the rebel armies were also helped indirectly by an internal struggle between Mongol factions in the north. One of the rebel leaders, the ex-monk Chu Yüan-chang (1328–98), eventually seized Khanbaliq, expelling the Mongols and bringing the Yüan dynasty to an end (1368).

While Chu Yüan-chang established himself as the first emperor of the Ming or Brilliant dynasty (1368–1644) in the new capital Nanking, the disgraced Toghon, who had barely escaped with his life to the Gobi, recorded his sorrow for posterity in a much-celebrated 'Lament' (in Mongolian) which is his only claim to fame. The ex-emperor died two years later in Mongolia. Only two months before his death Pope Urban V, unaware of these developments, had appointed a new mission to Khanbaliq led by the French Minorite William Desprès (March 1370). This embassy never reached its destination and its fate is unknown.

The end of Mongol rule in China and the national restoration inevitably brought about the downfall of the alien interests and the religious groups that had been closely associated with the Mongol régime. Christianity in all its forms was one of the victims of this wave of xenophobia, but its extinction was perhaps more the result of forced assimilation than outright persecution. An interesting document ascribed to the Dominican John (de Galonifontibus?), Archbishop of Sultanieh from 1398 to 1401, hints at the existence of Christians still in Cathay at the end of the fourteenth century. After this all too vague indication nothing more is heard about them. Completely cut off from the West, the foreign Christian community in China gradually blended into the native Chinese population, its churches falling into ruin or being converted into Buddhist temples. By the time the famous Jesuit missionary Matteo Ricci of Macerata (1552–1610) arrived in China in 1583 no traces were left of the early Franciscan mission and, to the end of his days, Ricci was not aware that Peking, only two and a half centuries earlier, had been the see of a Catholic Archbishop.

Of the very few material remains of this early mission that have come to light in modern times the tombstone of Catherine Vilioni is unquestionably the most important. There are, however, two more objects that probably belong to the same epoch. One, the so-called 'Bible of Marco Polo', is a thirteenth-century Bible in Latin, of north Italian origin, found in China in the seventeenth century and kept now in the Biblioteca Medicea Laurenziana in Florence, where it is in a state of complete decay. Its former Chinese owner claimed that it had been in his family since the Yüan dynasty, and it is indeed possible that it had originally belonged to one of the Franciscan missionaries.

The other object is a Latin chalice made in China, now in the treasure of the Church of St. Mark in Venice. Judging by the Mongol-style scenes in relief, it may also date from the thirteenth or fourteenth century.

If we had to rely merely on this meagre evidence and on the Mongol and Chinese sources, we would know nothing about the Franciscan travellers and their epic journeys to the court of the Great Khan. Fortunately, their letters and reports have come down to us and they make as interesting and exciting reading today as they did five centuries ago.

Epilogue

The Mongols' encounter with higher civilizations in Persia and China, and their khans' conversion to Islam and Buddhism, had the effect of rapidly eroding the weak ideological foundations on which their nomadic empire was built. Internal strife between conservative and progressive elements within the ruling élite of the khanates and the Mongols' unsound economic policies hastened the inevitable process of political disintegration.

The break-up of the Ilkhanid state and the internal collapse of the Golden Horde in the second half of the fourteenth century brought to an end the already much reduced activity of the missionaries, and closed at the same time the land route to European merchants and travellers to the East. The conquests of Timur Lang, our Tamerlane (1336–1405), and the definitive victory of Islam in Central Asia that followed them further isolated Europe from Asia.

In China the shock caused by the Mongol domination induced a mood of political isolation and cultural introspection which was to last for several centuries. During the thirteenth and fourteenth centuries China had, in effect, been a province of the 'greater' Mongol empire which stretched from eastern Europe to the China Sea, and it was this aspect of political geography, more than the so-called Pax Mongolica, that made possible the journeys to Cathay of Marco Polo and the Franciscan travellers. However, as far as China was concerned, the impact of these Western merchants and missionaries on the native culture, with which they had no real contact, was insignificant. Kublai no doubt enjoyed listening to Marco Polo's stories about Europe, but none of the information on the West supplied by his Venetian protégé found its way into any of the Chinese or Mongolian historical works. Not even Marco Polo's name seems to have been recorded in any contemporary source; at least, so far it has not turned up. Official historiography was firmly in the hands of Chinese bureaucrats who believed that most 'tribute-bearing foreigners' were not important or reliable enough to warrant inclusion in works for posterity.

On the other hand, outside the narrow-minded and traditionally supercilious official circle, Chinese scholarship was not impervious to outside influences. In sharp contrast to the scanty information on the Western Regions found in the official sources we have, for instance, a superb fourteenth-century Sino-Korean map of the world showing Africa, already with its characteristic triangular shape and pointing southwards, and Europe with about a hundred localities identified by name.

This map, by far superior to all contemporary European world maps, was compiled on the basis of information supplied by Western, almost certainly Arabic or Persian, sources. But isolated achievements like this, and the selective adoption of certain western Asian techniques, especially in the field of astronomy, did not affect in the least the Chinese outlook of the world in which China, whether ruled by a native or by a foreign dynasty, invariably occupied the central position, with everywhere else forming an ill-defined outlying zone of barbarian settlements.

After the fall of the Yüan, even the meaning of the word *Fu-lang* or Frank, the current designation of Europeans in the Mongol period, was soon forgotten. In the early sixteenth century this word reappeared in the form *Fo-lang-chi*, i.e.

Farangi or Frangi, introduced from Malaya, but it was at first applied only to the Western artillery, much as we use 'franc' to designate certain currencies. It was only later (after 1517) that the term was applied to the Portuguese, but as they had reached China from Malacca the Chinese believed that the 'Kingdom of the Franks' was now somewhere in southeast Asia, and that the Franks were a variety of Indians, a belief further confirmed by the Buddhist garb worn by the first Jesuit missionaries in the latter part of the century. Thus Europe was transposed to Asia in a way that reminds one of Europe's earlier translation of Prester John's kingdom from Asia to Africa.

In Europe the interruption of direct contacts with the Far East in the fifteenth century did not stop people from dreaming and speculating about the fabulous realms described by Marco Polo and Sir John Mandeville. Among literate and illiterate alike, the image of Asia in this period was that curious blend of facts and fiction epitomized by Mandeville's imaginative *Travels*.

With the revival of traditional and fabulous themes about the Orient some important facts were forgotten, among them the equivalence of Marco Polo's Cathay with China. It was only in 1575 that the Spanish Augustinian missionary Martín de Rada recognized that China was Cathay, although Matteo Ricci, who reached the same conclusion independently a few years later, is usually given the credit.

If the pioneer Franciscan explorers were soon forgotten, the rich mass of information that they had gathered in their reports was not lost. Much of it, as we have already seen, was incorporated in the works of their great contemporaries Vincent of Beauvais and Roger Bacon. Moreover, their discoveries and observations were not ignored by the cartographers and geographers of the Renaissance, as shown by the toponymy and representations of the Eastern regions of the world in the Venetian planispheres, the *Catalan Atlas* and the recently discovered, and still very controversial, *Vinland Map*.

Thus, the early papal envoys and missionaries who for the first time revealed to an astonished Europe the real wonders of Asia were, with Marco Polo, the precursors of that age of great maritime explorations and discoveries which was to have such momentous consequences for both continents in the following centuries.

RITTER LIBRARY
BALDWIN WALLACE COLLEGE

Bibliography

INTRODUCTORY NOTE

The best critical edition of the original Latin texts of the Franciscans' narratives is found in Volume I of A. van den Wyngaert, *Sinica Franciscana*. All of them are now available in English. For John of Pian di Carpine, William of Rubruck and John of Montecorvino the reader can avail himself of the accurate and eminently readable translations 'by a Nun of Stanbrook Abbey' in Christopher Dawson's *The Mongol Mission*. Incidentally, this book also contains translations of Benedict the Pole's short account, the letters of Peregrine of Castello and Andrew of Perugia, as well as a translation of Güyüg's letter in Persian to Pope Innocent IV. A new translation of this famous letter made by Professor J. A. Boyle of Manchester University will be found in the Appendix of the present volume.

Benedict's longer version, as recorded by Friar C. de Bridia, is edited and translated in R. A. Skelton, T. E. Marston, and G. Painter, *The Vinland Map and the Tartar Relation*.

Both Odoric of Pordenone and John of Marignolli have been translated and annotated by Sir Henry Yule in Volumes II and III of his still invaluable *Cathay and the Way Thither*.

The text of Simon of St. Quentin's report of Friar Ascelinus' mission has been edited with a useful commentary by J. Richard (*Histoire des Tartares*), but without translation.

For the general history of the period one may consult the works of C. D'Ohsson, R. Grousset and the other authors cited in the Bibliography. Unfortunately a good and comprehensive history of the Mongols is still lacking. H. H. Howorth's monumental *History of the Mongols from the 9th to the 19th Century* (London, 1876–88) is not reliable and is, in many ways, inferior to the earlier work by D'Ohsson.

The best general survey of European-Mongol relations in the thirteenth and fourteenth centuries is still G. Soranzo, *Il Papato, l'Europa cristiana e i Tartari*. However, the reader will find that Leonardo Olschki's delightful books (listed in the Bibliography) provide an excellent commentary to most of the historical, literary and geographical questions raised in the present volume which, for reasons of space, I have not been able to discuss in detail.

Only the most essential and easily available works are listed in the Bibliography. For further reading a useful work of reference is D. Sinor, *Introduction à l'étude de l'Eurasie Centrale*, Harrassowitz, Wiesbaden, 1963.

ALTANER, B. *Die Dominikanermissionen des 13. Jahrhunderts*, Breslauer Studien zur historischen Theologie, Bd. 3, Habelschwerdt, 1924.

BARTHOLD, V. V. *Turkestan down to the Mongol Invasion*, trans. by H. A. R. Gibb, 2nd ed. rev., Luzac, London, 1958.

BOYLE, J. A. (ed.). *The Cambridge History of Iran*. Vol. V: *The Saljuq and Mongol Periods*, Cambridge University Press, 1968.

BRETSCHNEIDER, E. *Mediaeval Researches from Eastern Asiatic Sources*, 2 vols., Kegan Paul, London, 1888; 2nd ed., London, 1910.

BUDGE, E. A. W. *The Monks of Kûblâi Khân, Emperor of China*, The Religious Tract Society, London, 1928.

CARY, G. *The Medieval Alexander*, Cambridge University Press, 1956; rep. 1967.

CORDIER, H. *Les voyages en Asie au XIVe siècle du bienheureux frère Odoric de Pordenone*, Leroux, Paris, 1891.

DAUVILLIER, J. 'Les Provinces Chaldéennes "de l'Extérieur" au Moyen Age', in *Mélanges F. Cavallera*, Toulouse, 1948, pp. 261–316.

DAWSON, C. (ed.). *The Mongol Mission. Narratives and Letters of the Franciscan Missionaries in Mongolia and China in the Thirteenth and Fourteenth Centuries*, trans. by a Nun of Stanbrook Abbey, Sheed and Ward, London and New York, 1955.

D'OHSSON, C. *Histoire des Mongols dépuis Tchinguiz-khan jusqu'à Timour Bey ou Tamerlan*, 4 vols., Les Frères van Cleef, La Haye et Amsterdam, 1834–35; ph. rep. Tientsin, 1940.

FRANKE, H. 'Sino-Western Contacts under the Mongol Empire', *Journal of the Hong Kong Branch of the Royal Asiatic Society* 6 (1966), pp. 49–72.

FRANKE, O. *Geschichte des chinesischen Reiches*, Vols. IV and V, W. de Gruyter, Berlin, 1948–52.

GOLUBOVICH, G. *Biblioteca bio-bibliografica della Terra Santa e dell'Oriente Francescano*, Vols. I–V, Collegio di S. Bonaventura, Quaracchi-Firenze, 1906–27.

GROUSSET, R. *Histoire des Croisades et du Royaume Franc de Jérusalem*, 3 vols., Plon, Paris, 1934–36.

L'Empire des Steppes: Attila, Gengis-khan, Tamerlan, Payot, Paris, 1939; rep. 1948.

Conqueror of the World, trans. by D. Sinor and M. MacKellar, Oliver and Boyd, Edinburgh and London, 1967.

HAENISCH, E. (tr.). *Die Geheime Geschichte der Mongolen*, 2nd ed., Harrassowitz, Leipzig, 1949.

HEISSIG, W. *A Lost Civilization. The Mongols Rediscovered*, trans. by D. J. S. Thomson, Thames and Hudson, London, 1956.

HENNIG, R. *Terrae Incognitae*, 4 vols., 2nd ed., E. J. Brill, Leiden, 1944–56.

Is.M.E.O. (ed.). *Oriente Poliano. Studi e conferenze tenute all'Istituto Italiano per il Medio ed Estremo Oriente, in occasione del VII Centenario della nascita di Marco Polo (1254–1954)*, Roma, 1957.

JORDAN OF SÉVÉRAC. See Jordanus Catalani.

JORDANUS CATALANI. *Mirabilia Descripta. The Wonders of the East*, trans. by H. Yule, The Hakluyt Society, London, 1863.

JUVAINI, 'Ala-ad-Din 'Ata-Malik. *The History of the World-Conqueror*, trans. by J. A. Boyle, 2 vols., Manchester University Press, 1958.

LACH, D. F. *Asia in the Making of Europe*, Vol. I in two, The University of Chicago Press, 1965.

LATTIMORE, O. *Inner Asian Frontiers of China*, 2nd ed., American Geographical Society, New York, 1951.
'Chingis Khan and the Mongol Conquests', *Scientific American* 209 (Aug. 1963), pp. 55–68.

LATTIMORE, O. and E. (ed.). *Silk, Spices, and Empire. Asia Seen through the Eyes of its Discoverers*, Delacorte Press, New York, 1968.

LETTS, M. (ed. and tr.). *Mandeville's Travels. Texts and Translations*, 2 vols., The Hakluyt Society, London, 1953.

LI CHIH-CH'ANG. *The Travels of an Alchemist. The Journey of the Taoist Ch'ang-ch'un from China to the Hindukush at the Summons of Chingiz Khan Recorded by His Disciple Li Chih-ch'ang*, trans. by A. Waley, George Routledge and Sons, London, 1931; rep. 1963.

MANDEVILLE, Sir J. *Travels*, see Letts.

MARCO POLO. *The Description of the World*, see Moule and Pelliot, and Yule.

MOULE, A. C. *Christians in China before the Year 1550*, Society for Promoting Christian Knowledge, London, 1930.

MOULE, A. C. and PELLIOT, P. *Marco Polo, The Description of the World*, 2 vols., George Routledge and Sons, London, 1938.

OLSCHKI, L. *Marco Polo's Precursors*, Johns Hopkins Press, Baltimore, 1943.
Guillaume Boucher. A French Artist at the Court of the Khans, Johns Hopkins Press, Baltimore, 1946.
Marco Polo's Asia. An Introduction to His 'Description of the World' Called 'Il Milione', trans. by J. A. Scott, The University of California Press, Berkeley and Los Angeles, 1960.

PELLIOT, P. *Notes on Marco Polo*, Vols. I–II, Adrien-Maisonneuve, Paris, 1959–63.
'Les Mongols et la Papauté', *Revue de l'Orient chrétien* 23 (1922–23), pp. 1–28; 24 (1924), pp. 225–335; 28 (1931–32), pp. 3–84.

PETECH, L. 'Les marchands italiens dans l'empire mongol', *Journal Asiatique* 250 (1962), pp. 549–74.

PHILLIPS, E. D. *The Mongols*, Thames and Hudson, London, 1969.

PLAN CARPIN, J. DE. *Histoire des Mongols*, trans. by Dom J. Becquet and L. Hambis, Adrien-Maisonneuve, Paris, 1965.

ROCKHILL, W. W. *The Journey of William of Rubruck to the Eastern Parts of the World, 1253–55, as Narrated by Himself with Two Accounts of The Earlier Journey of John of Pian de Carpine*, The Hakluyt Society, London, 1900.

RUNCIMAN, S. *A History of the Crusades*, 3 vols., Cambridge University Press, 1952–54.

SAINT-QUENTIN, S. DE. *Histoire des Tartares*, ed. by J. Richard, Paul Geuthner, Paris, 1965.

SINOR, D. 'Les relations entre les Mongols et l'Europe jusqu'à la mort d'Arghoun et de Béla IV', *Cahiers d'histoire mondiale* 3 (1956), pp. 39–61.

SKELTON, R. A., MARSTON, T. E., and PAINTER, G. D. *The Vinland Map and the Tartar Relation*, Yale University Press, New Haven and London, 1965.

SLESSAREV, V. *Prester John. The Letter and the Legend*, University of Minneapolis Press, 1959.

SORANZO, G. *Il Papato, l'Europa cristiana e i Tartari. Un secolo di penetrazione occidentale in Asia*, Università Cattolica del Sacro Cuore, Milano, 1930.

SPULER, B. *Die Goldene Horde. Die Mongolen in Russland, 1223–1502*, 2nd ed., Harrassowitz, Wiesbaden, 1965.

VERNADSKY, G. *The Mongols and Russia*, Yale University Press, New Haven, 1953.

VLADIMIRTSOV, B. *Le régime social des Mongols. Le féodalisme nomade*, trans. by M. Carsow, Adrien-Maisonneuve, Paris, 1948.

WALEY, A. *The Secret History of the Mongols and Other Pieces*, George Allen and Unwin, London, 1963.

WYNGAERT, A. VAN DEN. *Sinica Franciscana*. Vol. I: *Itinera et relationes Fratrum Minorum saeculi XIII et XIV*, Collegio di S. Bonaventura, Quaracchi-Firenze, 1929; ph. rep. 1962.

YULE, H. *Cathay and the Way Thither, Being a Collection of Medieval Notices of China*, 4 vols., new ed., rev. The Hakluyt Society, London, 1913–16; rep. by Kraus Reprint Ltd., Nendeln/Liechtenstein, 1967. *The Book of Ser Marco Polo the Venetian Concerning the Kingdoms and Marvels of the East*, 2 vols., 3rd ed. revised by H. Cordier, John Murray, London, 1903. To use concurrently with H. Cordier's *Ser Marco Polo. Notes and Addenda to Sir Henry Yule's Edition, Containing the Results of Recent Research and Discovery*, John Murray, London, 1920.

Appendix

The Letter of the Great Khan Güyüg to Pope Innocent IV (1246) *

By the power of the Eternal Sky, [We] the Oceanic Khan of the whole great people; Our command.†

This is an order sent to the great Pope that he may know and understand it.

We have written it in the language of the lands of the *kerel* (i.e. Latin?).

Counsel was held; a petition of submission was sent; it was heard from your ambassadors.

And if you keep to your word, thou, who art the great Pope, together with all the kings, must come in person to do homage to Us. We shall then cause you to hear every command that there is of the *Yasa* ('Law').

Again. You have said: 'Become Christian, it will be good.' Thou hast made thyself wise (*or* thou hast been presumptuous); thou hast sent a petition. This petition of thine We have not understood.

Again. You have sent words [saying]: 'Thou hast taken all the lands of the Majar and the Christians; I am astonished. What was their crime? Tell us.' These words of thine We have not understood either. The command of God, Chingiz Khan and Qa'an (= Ögödei), both of them, sent it to cause it to be heard. They have not trusted the command of God. Just like thy words they too have been reckless; they have acted with arrogance; and they killed Our ambassadors. The people of those countries, [it was] the Ancient God [who] killed and destroyed them. Except by the command of God, how should anyone kill, how should [anyone] capture by his own strength?

Dost thou say none the less: 'I am a Christian; I worship God; I despise and . . .'?‡ How dost thou know whom God forgives, to whom He shows mercy? How dost thou know, who speakest such words?

* This is a new translation, kindly prepared by Prof. J. A. Boyle, of the Persian letter in the Vatican Archives (see above, p. 103). As the original text is faulty in several places, the present translation cannot, however, be regarded as definitive.

† This preamble is in Turkish.

‡ This phrase is incomplete and its meaning is not clear. According to P. Pelliot ('Les Mongols et la Papauté', 1922–23, pp. 20–21, n. 7) it probably contained a reference to the Nestorian Christians.

By the power of God [from] the going up of the sun to [his] going down [He] has delivered all the lands to Us; We hold them. Except by the command of God, how can anyone do [anything]? Now you must say with a sincere heart: 'We shall become [your] subjects; we shall give [our] strength.' Thou in person at the head of the kings, you must all together at once come to do homage to Us. We shall then recognize your submission. And if you do not accept God's command and act contrary to Our command We shall regard you as enemies.

Thus We inform you. And if you act contrary [thereto], what do We know [of it], [it is] God [who] knows.

In the last days of Jumādā II of the year six hundred and forty-four (3-11 November 1246).

Index

215

230

RITTER LIBRARY
BALDWIN-WALLACE COLLEGE

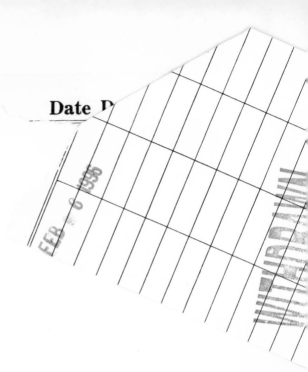

Date D

FEB 0 1996

WITHDRAWN